Copula

SUNY series in Gender Theory

Tina Chanter, editor

Copula

Sexual Technologies, Reproductive Powers

Robyn Ferrell

STATE UNIVERSITY OF NEW YORK PRESS

Published by
State University of New York Press, Albany

Printed in the United States of America

For information, address State University of New York Press,
194 Washington Avenue, Suite 305, Suite 700, Albany, NY 12210-2384

Production by Kelli Williams
Marketing by Anne M. Valentine

Library of Congress Cataloging-in-Publication Data

Ferrell, Robyn, 1960–
Copula : sexual technologies, reproductive powers / Robyn Ferrell.
p. cm.
Includes bibliographical references and index.
ISBN 0-7914-6753-8 (hardcover : alk. paper)—ISBN 0-7914-6754-6 (pbk. : alk. paper)
1. Sex role–Philosophy. 2. Feminist theory. 3. Motherhood—Philosophy. I. Title.

HQ1075.F474 2006
306.874'3'01–dc22 2005020543

10 9 8 7 6 5 4 3 2 1

For my mother, Pat
For my son, David

Contents

Preface

The advent of feminism in an intellectual history of the twentieth century is not surprising, but on the contrary can be taken too much for granted. Consider the advent of feminism at the same time as the explosion of technology; feminism at the same time as the rearrangement of the family and the means of reproduction; feminism at the same time as an inclusive political rationality—democracy—grows in company with a mass consumerism that is desiring to the point of violence. Feminism is a product as much as an agent of these times.

Feminism is kin to technology. This book endeavors to show this through reflection on the reproductive technologies, among other things. Technology produces change, sometimes dramatic change, in the material world and its innovation can be seen to exceed the thought that engendered it. I argue that this is not only a property of technology but indeed of *any reproduction.* The concept of reproduction, like that of technology, involves a paradox. In reproduction, something is produced of a kind that was there before and yet that is also new; reproduction must produce that which is "the same, only different" (Lacy 2000). The paradox arising in the concept of technology is most eloquently put by Heidegger: "[T]he essence of technology is by no means anything technological" (1977, 287). Technology, while being the most material of events—indeed it is definitive of materialism—is first and foremost a "way of thinking."

The logic of paradox is an important contributor to the strangeness engendered by the reproductive technologies. In examining the context in which this strangeness arises, this study encounters some central convictions about the nature of human life and love, convictions governed by the paradox of the relations between oneself and others. This social reality, which is an affective climate so strong that it can induce joy and despair in each of us, appears on reflection to be strangely compliant with the conceptual relation of subject to object.

When understood as a grammatical structure, the distinction between subject and object gives us the attribution of identity per se: "I am that." And when analyzed as a logical relation, the difference between subject and object turns out to produce distinction *as such*. This is the figure I have isolated as the copula, in its logical, linguistic, and sexual resonances. My discussion draws on scholarship in feminist theory, philosophy of technology, psychoanalytic theory, ethics, anthropology, history, and other social sciences for the material of its reflection. But it is not an empirical exercise—it is a study of the conceptual schema underlying our present understanding of these technologies. One of the main directions of its analysis is into the conceptual isomorphism between social, psychical, linguistic, and logical dimensions that provide a particular background of thought to the question of technology.

Chapter 1 begins from the often unacknowledged role in reproduction of maternity. The maternal is the ground on which the reproductive technologies enact their change. But this cannot be a simple mechanical graft, considering the many deep meanings of the maternal. In "The Maternal in Its Natural Habitat," the feminist analysis of the maternal as an unexamined ground for the figure of the modern subject is explored for what it might reveal of this logical inquiry into technological thought. The work of psychoanalytic feminists is reviewed as one of the few serious revisions of the place of the maternal as exempted and silenced. Yet, the psychical configurations around it are only part of the story, when one reflects on the features of maternity that inhibit women in practice, the most glaring of these in a modern economy being the labor of mothering.

The effect of feminism may have been to release women from the inevitability of maternity, but it is concluded that this has not changed the burden of the maternal in the contemporary scheme of things. Indeed, the commodity-style of thought engendered by the technological appears to intensify the maternal as an abjected and unacknowledged grounding for the subject. It is not unreasonable to ask why feminism has so far failed to change the conditions under which reproduction is carried out, but has only served to displace the burden from literal mothers to other women who function as surrogates.

In turning to the specific question of the reproductive technologies, the second chapter, "Brave New World," looks toward a future engendered by these technologies and their excesses. The reproductive technologies as a source of ethical reflection for contemporary "bioethics" is contrasted with the desires inherent in their realization. Both the desire and the horror of these technologies is engendered by their relation to the future, itself a concept governed by paradox. The chapter proceeds by scrutinizing the "aporia" of paradox, and advocating the *risk* that the future, embodied in technology, demands we take on.

In chapter 3, "Reproducing Technology," I look at the conventional feminist ethical and political arguments concerning reproductive technology but conclude that none of them attempt to understand the issue as an ontological one, with the result that their depictions of the future offered by these technologies is often unconvincing. Part of this failure is identified as coming from the failure to understand feminism as itself a kind of thinking, and its own relation to rationality. Understanding feminism as itself a technology, that is, as a kind of thought whose conceptions—equality for women, for example—have become material events, throws new light on the reproductive technologies. It raises the possibility that the theory that utilizes the social sciences, no less than the life sciences, might bring its objects of analysis to life.

Chapter 4, "Conceiving of Feminism," looks in detail at the styles of thought underpinning the action of certain kinds of feminism, including "feminism of equality" and "radical feminism." It argues that despite their differences, these theories fail to challenge the dichotomies that set sexual difference, as a system of subordination, in motion. The attempt to confine feminism to a rationality, even one with a literary sensibility, can be seen—for example, in the work of Michele le Doeuff—as an intellectual truncation that leaves feminist thinking prey to its own illusions.

Some "feminism of difference," however, has turned its thought toward the category of difference and thereby into the study of the metaphysical thinking that governs the times. In chapter 5, "Feminism Is a Kind of Time," several of the conceptual consequences of that reflection are opened up. The focus of this theory is on the conceptual opposition of the masculine and the feminine, as both a critical symbolic formation in metaphysical thinking and a crucial psychical support in the life of the subject.

Much contemporary feminist theory engages the general critiques of rationality advanced in the philosophy of the subject, using theorists from phenomenological, psychoanalytic, and deconstructive perspectives. Chapter 6, "The Lore of the Father," examines elements in these metaphysical debates that have produced both useful outcomes and treacherous encounters for feminist theorists. The critique of the logic of distinction offered in these traditions is frequently gender-blind. And yet, when the analysis is brought to the case of sexual difference, many questions about difference in general can be clarified.

In chapter 7, "The Figure of the Copula," the structure of a subject distinguished from its objects is analyzed in its grammatical, logical, social, and erotic incarnations. The resulting oppositional thinking can be seen to produce effects across this spectrum that, while dramatically unlike in life, have a similar diagnosis. Deconstruction and other methods for understanding the logic of distinction can be brought to bear both on the logical difficulty of clearly distinguishing a subject from its predicates, and on the social reality of marriage and erotic domination.

The isomorphism of the copula in these modes of thought is a curious product of the intertwining of the material and the conceptual, an intertwining that is the very property of the technological. The body itself is the first technology in this sense, imbued as it is with signification both as a subjective entity and as it appears for others. In chapter 8, "The Body as Material Event," several analyses of why this should be so are explored, focusing on the psychoanalytic account of the origin of thought in the drives of the body, and phenomenological accounts of the engendering of bodily difference through habitual interaction with other bodies.

Chapter 9, "The Technology of Genre," puts forward the analysis of technology made by Heidegger in the context of his wider aesthetics in which worlds are formed. But the question posed specifically by the reproductive technologies which is not anticipated in Heidegger is the consequence of a kind of thinking directed at sexual difference. Technology, conceived as a kind of thinking, issues from a rationality that is recognizably Western and metaphysical. But it is also, in the manner of the aesthetic, a kind of thought that engenders transformation. I argue the concept of a "technology of genre" would use an approach to discourse that helps to render the problem of reproduction, sexual difference, and technology as part of the more general inquiry into representation as a force that changes things.

Acknowledgements

Many people have helped with the preparation of this book. I would like to thank in particular, Tina Chanter, Kelly Oliver, Moira Gatens, Elspeth Probyn, Ros Diprose, Pene Deutscher, Karen Throsby, Jennifer Biddle, Ewa Ziarek and Linnell Secomb. I would also like to thank my students from Macquarie University and the University of Tasmania, for their contribution in discussion.

I would like to acknowledge the support of the Australian Research Council for research time in which to complete the project, and the Gender Institute of the London School of Economics and Political Science for periods spent as a visiting scholar there while working on this material.

Earlier versions of some parts of the following chapters have appeared previously, viz:

- "Desire and Horror: Conceiving of the Future," in *Borderlands* e-journal, Vol. 3 No. 1, 2004.
- "The Pleasures of the Slave," in *Between the Psyche and the Social*, ed. Kelly Oliver and Steve Edwin (Lanham, MD: Rowman & Littlefield, 2002).
- "Copula: Feminism and the Sexual Relation," in *Hypatia* (15) 2, 2000 special issue on "Going Australian" conference, ed. C. Battersby, R. Jones, and C. Constable.
- "Two Figures of Feminism and Philosophy," in Max Deutscher, ed., *Michele le Doeuff: Operative Philosophy and Imaginary Practice* (New York: Humanity Books, 2000).
- "The Time of Feminism," in *Hypatia* (14) 1, 1999.
- "The Lore of the Father," in *Hypatia* (6) 3, 1991.

ONE

The Maternal in Its Natural Habitat

> . . . the murderous alternation between bitter resentment and raw-edged nerves, and blissful gratification and tenderness. Sometimes I seem to myself, in my feelings toward these tiny guiltless beings, a monster of selfishness and intolerance. Their voices wear away at my nerves, their constant needs, above all their need for simplicity and patience, fill me with despair at my own failures, despair too at my fate, which is to serve a function for which I was not fitted. And I am weak sometimes from held-in rage . . .
>
> And yet at other times I am melted with the sense of their helpless, charming and quite irresistible beauty—their ability to go on loving and trusting . . . *I love them.*
>
> —Adrienne Rich, *Of Woman Born*

Gender has been reworked and qualified, and sexuality has been reordered, so that the first statements of feminists about the oppression of the feminine may seem today rather dated. Feminist theory has played its part in the dramatic reshaping of women's lives with men, and with other women; workforce participation, financial enfranchisement, inclusion in public institutions (including the university), pursuit of pleasures.

But women's relations with children? Perhaps the fact that many more women are today sole parents might count as a "dramatic reshaping," but it wasn't an aspiration of the movement. And still, the first "second wave" statements on maternity remain sharply observed, unchanged, and unqualified. Women, even in the Western world, are still overwhelmingly responsible for child rearing. It is striking that when one looks back to literature considered to be at the inception of the present movement—for example, Adrienne Rich's *Of Woman Born*—one still finds the material there as fresh as ever.

Readers of Kristeva and Irigaray and their commentators may feel affronted at the assertion that there has "been no progress" in theory on motherhood. What about the analyses offered by psychoanalytic feminisms? But by "progress" I mean the accommodation of maternity into an intellectual practice, or even into a feminist practice. This has not happened. As Susan Maushart writes, in *The Masks of Motherhood*: "Feminism has only allowed women to evade maternity" (and cf. MacCannell 2000, 154). It has not taught women how to engage with maternity, in the way we have engaged with the production of other sites of our difference, in order to challenge them.

There has been "progress" in other practices of maternity. It is precisely as progress that the developments in the reproductive technologies are presently accelerating—as the inevitable destiny or, at the very least as the unstoppable temptation, of the technological world. The absence of a maternal *ontology* is a cause of anxiety—it should concern us that technology is supervening on a maternity that is not yet a feminist *habitus.*

Perhaps the reason for this is, on a practical level, depressingly simple. Most women must still choose between being mothers and theorists. The academy, where most theorizing is done and all theory must presently be enfranchised, is still designed along the traditional lines. It is a model of labor supported by a care-giving function performed elsewhere by someone else. This "professional" model of intellectual work assumes that academics can disappear into the library for hours at a time, stay late to teach their classes, hop off to conferences, and adjourn to the bar for congenial collegial linkage—which, as well as being pleasurable, cements the patronage of referees and publishing opportunities—finally to burn the midnight oil writing things down.

The effect of women working in the labor force, including the intellectual labor force, has been to highlight the "vulgar Marxist" point, that the circumstances that have prevented women from entering the workforce previously are not properties peculiar to gender, but a simple calculus of actions—women have been tied up doing something else, and in most cases looking after other people. Motherhood is that part of being a woman that is least amenable to the demands of intellectual labor. This is not because a mother cannot think—it is not a case of the old gynecologists' lore that a woman "gives birth to her brain." Anyone who has had the care of a child, and has done it conscientiously, knows there is no possibility of thinking sustained thought or losing oneself in concentration—care giving as a practise is extrovert in the extreme.

Indeed, as styles of labor, maternal and intellectual labor are almost diametrically opposed: one demands extroversion and action, and is contingent on circumstances to a high degree; the other is solipsistic, autonomous, and sustained. Consequently, the fantasy of being able to write while the baby is asleep is just that.

Actually, what this reveals is theory as *itself* a kind of labor, that is to say a kind of action, which is also to say that it is an aspect of *embodiment.* This embodiment may be effaced in its product, but is critical to its possibility. Intellectual labor is embodied to a very high degree, in that it demands becoming absorbed in the task to the exclusion of all else. It is not only that it is not possible to do philosophy while being a mother; it is also that it is not possible to do *anything else* while doing philosophy. But: "I can't do two things at once"—how often does one hear a mother say this?

Concentration on the task is a kind of focus that engages the whole being. This brings it close to the paradigm case of labor, as Marx imagines it in the *Grundrisse,* as the inalienable expression of the body's action. If it turns out that maternity and philosophy are incompatible—if "mother theory" is a contradiction in terms—it will be, ironically, because both are such pure forms of this unalienated labor.

And, seen in such terms, two possibilities might be explored. Firstly, that despite the undeniable wisdom in psychoanalytic observation, the "two-in-one" subjectivity of pregnancy is not the best emblem of maternity. Once a child is born, it becomes for the mother a more pressing case of *labor relations.* But secondly, the "two-in-one" conundrum of maternal identity may suggest that a different ontology is proposed by maternity, one in which a complication of the subject/object relation, and therefore of the whole mode of thinking that underwrites conventional ontologies, could be reconceived.

PHILOSOPHY'S MYTH OF ORIGIN

No doubt, there is as yet no mother theory in philosophy, because these two terms are nearly oxymoronic. One apparently refers to a natural state—indeed, the epitome of the natural. Maternity is about as natural as the human gets, in contact with its species-being, confronted by it.

Theory, on the contrary, is that ethereal production, the highest of cultural values, the most extruded and abstracted, even abstruse, state of humanity, its most *unnatural* act. So philosophers pride themselves upon; so they like to think. The ontology of the human is thinking, we are the thinking being, says Heidegger on our behalf.

Hume allows us a challenging possibility, not much explored, when he writes in the *Enquiry*: "A blind man can form no notion of colours; a deaf man of sounds." If we are not "susceptible" to any species of sensation, then we lack susceptibility to the idea. Similarly, where an object or agent of sensation has never been met with, the idea is absent: "A Laplander or Negro has no notion of the relish of wine." And this is true, by extension, for the affective realm, too: "A man of mild manners can form no idea of inveterate revenge or cruelty; nor can a selfish heart easily conceive the heights of friendship and generosity" (but cf. my argument in Ferrell 2002). This conception of thought makes it an experience, empirical in principle—"the only manner by which an idea can have access to the mind, to wit by the actual feeling and sensation" (ibid.). If mothers were also ontologists, then they might think differently from other philosophers.

Had de Beauvoir, for example, been a mother, she may not have observed one to be "taking her leisure" at the park with the infant. Simone de Beauvoir, childless and yet the mother of modern feminism, accepts the story about the privilege of philosophy lying outside natural states, and shares the conviction that maternity could never be philosophy.

Rejecting the prejudice that biology is destiny, de Beauvoir cites contraception as a demonstration that reproduction is not "at the mercy solely of biological chance" (501). But the choice to interrupt reproduction is the last expression of freedom the mother-to-be might make. "For she does not really make the baby, it makes itself within her; her flesh engenders flesh only . . . " and, "Ordinary life is but a condition of existence; in gestation it appears as creative; but that is a strange kind of creation which is accomplished in a contingent and passive manner."

The labor of the body is not of the same ontological order as the labor of the mind. "With her ego surrendered, alienated in her body and in her social dignity, the mother enjoys the comforting illusion of feeling that she is a human being *in herself, a value*. . . . But this is only an illusion" (514).

This is because maternity does not have the appropriate relation between subject and object—and this, by its essential equivocation; "[S]he and the child with which she is swollen make up together an equivocal pair, overwhelmed by life. Ensnared by nature, the pregnant woman is plant and animal . . ." (512).

This argument turns on a general, almost banal, commitment of the philosophical tradition, which seeks to differentiate the human from the animal-vegetal, on the ground of the mind-body distinction—its "thinking being," and even of a particular thinking being that can be described as "technological thinking being." That is to say, a style of thought that analyzes itself as capable of transcendence just because it is capable of insisting on the difference between itself as subject and its objects.

It isn't clear that this form of projection is the only form of thought there is. Indeed, even Heidegger, in reviewing *techne*, writes as though the category of creation is larger than the technological, although in danger of being overwhelmed by it. I don't need to labor the complaint already made against existential philosophy for its capture of de Beauvoir's thought. But I do need to dwell on it a little more, in order to bring into focus the ellision of maternity as essential in philosophy.

In attempting to answer the question of the *cause* of the inequality between the sexes, de Beauvoir tells us that: "This has always been a man's world, and none of the reasons hitherto brought forward in explanation of the fact has seemed adequate" (93). Dismissing the Marxist and the psychoanalytic accounts, she offers a myth of origin from the point of view of existentialism. "But we shall be able to understand how the hierarchy of the sexes was established by reviewing the data of prehistoric research and ethnography in the light of existentialist philosophy."

"The woman who gave birth did not feel the pride of creation; she felt herself the plaything of obscure forces"; "The primitive hordes had no permanence in property or territory, and hence set no store by posterity; children were for them a burden, not a prized possession"; "Even in times when humans most needed births, when maternity was most venerated, manual labour was the primary necessity." A fantastic portrait is offered, of feelings purported to have been felt by pre-agricultural woman thousands of years ago, but no doubt large also in the mind of the author. The story reflects any number of prejudices against maternity, but more particular is the definitional problem she presents for early woman: "But in any case giving birth and suckling are not *activities*, they are natural functions; no project is involved; and that is why woman found in them no reason for a lofty affirmation of her existence—she submitted passively to her biologic fate" (94).

A contrast is then drawn between maternal and masculine labor; "[H]e furnished support for the group, not in the manner of worker bees by a simple vital process, through biological behaviour, but by means of acts that transcended his animal nature" (95). His hunting is a creative act. "Man's activity had another dimension that gave it supreme dignity: it was often dangerous"; "life is not the supreme value for man, but on the contrary that it should be made to serve ends more important than itself"; "For it is not in giving life but in risking life that man is raised above the animal; that is why superiority has been accorded in humanity not to the sex that brings forth but to that which kills" (95–96). If there have been suspicions nurtured that de Beauvoir wrote much of Sartre's philosophy, we might here rather suspect that Sartre was writing de Beauvoir's.

This myth of origin is disturbing for feminism; One can wonder that misogyny engenders a new wave of feminist emancipation, and ask what values that feminism unconsciously has taken on from its conception. But for philosophy, on the other hand, the myth is humdrum; here is a summary of a whole history of philosophy which distinguishes humanity from animal life. It catches one up in discussion of human being, through a distinction within humanity between two kinds of human being, the sexes. Humanity becomes something that distinguishes itself *from* life, through a project rather than through a fate, in the terms of the myth. We have "the key to the whole mystery"; and the definition of humanity has played an important part in it.

This is a Platonic myth; the *counternatural* act defines the human. The perpetuation of life is a natural function according to de Beauvoir, according to the history of philosophy. But the taking of life, and the worship of death, even—these are the prerogatives that belong to humanity (read: to philosophy). Just as for Plato, in the *Symposium*, it is proper to philosophy to put aside even love for its own sake and use it in its tutelary function; so life will exceed itself in a transcendent imagining that specifies itself as beyond the merely lived.

We have become entangled in many myths of origin, not only of the sexual relation, but of human being and the thinking being, too. By this, we know the extent of the problem presented by maternity for philosophy, and the involvement of sexual difference generally in an ideal of rationality.

In some sense, the whole project of *The Second Sex* is undermined from here. Giving a liberatory account of the sex of woman can only now proceed by giving an account of her *as a man.* Because masculinity has been equated with humanity and humanity with rationality, what is left over of the human after rationality will be demoted to an animal function, and the second sex is by definition adjunctive.

Why is giving life any more natural than taking life? And must the discussion of sexual oppression proceed via affects of species pride? Take the example of the lioness; does she make the distinction, between biological function and project, when she suckles her cubs or slaughters the gazelle? Why is this story of de Beauvoir's so plausible, so that we overlook the extravagant interpretation made of the *natural* world, as one in which death takes priority over life, or the aggressive over the nurturant?

Just how does philosophy accomplish this transcendence? How is it that projects are not projections, or if they are, why are they not themselves "illusions"? And: Why is *philosophy* presented as an *existential* state at all? Why is philosophy too not understood as a kind of labor?

THE MATERNAL IN ITS NATURAL SETTING

Kelly Oliver has expressed the contradiction well, when she comments, in *Family Values*:

> But in both philosophy and psychoanalytic theory, it turns out that the paternal authority that legitimates culture and breaks with anti-social nature is founded on the father's *natural* authority because of his *natural* strength and aggressive impulses. The paternal authority of culture is founded on the father's naturally stronger body: might makes right. (1997, 5)

She further argues that the opposing of the maternal and paternal as distinctions between antisocial body and disembodied culture, which itself is a version of the mind/body distinction, renders love impossible: "Western images of conception, birth, and parental relationships leave us with a father who is not embodied, who cannot love but only legislates from some abstract position, and a mother who is nothing but body, who can fulfill animal needs but cannot love as a social human body" (3).

Oliver uses Kristeva, among other theorists, to provide the alternative of an embodied culture that allows for an ethics founded on love. And, of all contemporary accounts of sexual relations used or criticized by feminist theorists, Kristeva's is perhaps the most detailed and most rehearsed. Irigaray stimulates critique with her utopian and increasingly aphoristic engagements with sexual different and philosophy. But Kristeva labors over the elements that structure the present cultural scene, and has offered an analytic discourse on maternity which presents its profound opportunity as well as its burden.

Criticism of Kristeva's theory is generally directed at what is seen as her capture by psychoanalysis, whose structural descriptions are said to essentialize the mind/body and culture/nature splits. And it is true, as Oliver points out in the passage quoted above, that philosophy and psychoanalysis are both conventionally understood as one on this point.

But it isn't clear that Kristeva's description of the maternal as a semiotic space underpinning culture serves to uphold the opposition of mind to body so much as to implicate one in the other. Kristeva offers, for example, a possible *discourse* of maternity, one that would replace the fantasized comfort of the Virgin Mary with a secular recognition of maternity's infolding of identity in the other. (This argument is outlined by Ewa Ziarek, among others: cf. Ziarek 1992. Irigaray's elaboration of the need for a feminine divine explores a similar intuition.)

Psychoanalysis, maternity, and poetry are opportunities—if there can be a discourse of maternity, it is possible in the *fold* of maternity, in the problem of two-in-one of which the pregnant woman is living emblem. As Ziarek outlines it: "Unlike the clear separation of and noncoincidence between the signifier and the signified, the subject and the Other, the maternal body renders the fundamental notions of identity and difference strikingly insufficient—these crucial philosophical categories indeed no longer 'hold up.' Therefore, such an inescapable imprint of otherness makes the maternal body impure, turns it into a 'catastrophic fold of being.' " (Ziarek 1992, 102).

"Herethics" names an opportunity in motherhood for an "outlaw ethics," one "conceived in love and not law" (Oliver, 182–83). And pregnancy is an everyday metaphysical enigma, an indeterminacy in identity which proceeds within daily life without psychotic consequences or logical contradiction. (And see Iris Marion Young's more phenomenological critique in "Pregnant Embodiment" in Young 1990.)

The *discourse of maternity* would name not only a new ethical but a new discursive possibility, since it takes place differently around the subject/object distinction. This distinction is elsewhere in psychoanalytic theory analyzed as necessary to the logic of the "Symbolic." Even in other discursive worlds, such as that proposed in existentialism and discussed above, the subject produces a distinction from his objects, not just as a prelude to transcendence, but also to thought.

This may be why "object-relations theory" harbors an obsessive anxiety about the maternal and defining its proper place. All this may be unconscious, except in the work of Klein, whose mordant recounting of fantasy does not mistake the symbolic for the real (cf. Doane 1992) For Winnicott, Chodorow, and others in this tradition, the mother guarantees the subject's passage into the human social, that is, "distinctive" world, on pain of psychological disturbance. But from a general perspective one can see that this is a failure to understand the conceptual stakes in the subject/object distinction—a psychology premised on the governing "technological" ontology is already at the outset battling myopia.

Thus, even the important feminist work of Nancy Chodorow entrenches a sexual distinction that at the same time causes it concern. In *Family Structure and Feminine Personality*, she notes that the early experience of bonding is different for each sex, and explains personality differences in terms of it. She argues that "psychoanalytic" understandings of this, rather than the usual sociological, can be illuminating by outlining the structural, internalized "object-relations" underpinning personality, These are unconscious, but constitutional of personality (47), and lead her to her critique, which is that early object-relations for children in the Western nuclear family yield unworkable sexual differences.

Chodorow claims a psychoanalytic account can give an understanding of why sex difference is indelible without obliging one to subscribe to biological determinism (54). It allows her to offer discussion of more traditional societies, where ego strength is given in different, and by implication psychically healthier, contexts of connection. This may be mere nostalgia, but Chodorow's analysis allows her to raise the possibility that the modern personality is not the best suited to women's reproductive lives, which implies a critique of Western subjectivity as masculine in its very conceptuality (59).

> Women's biosexual experiences (menstruation, coitus, pregnancy, childbirth, lactation) all involve some challenge to the boundaries of her body ego ("me"/"not-me" in relation to her blood or milk, to a man who penetrates her, to a child once part of her body). These are important and fundamental human experiences that are probably intrinsically meaningful and at the same time complicated for women everywhere. However, a Western woman's tenuous sense of individuation and of the firmness of her ego boundaries increase the likelihood that experiences challenging these boundaries will be difficult for her and conflictual. (59)

This tenuousness, a personality trait, is produced by the arrangement of exclusive parenting by the mother, while the father exists as a fantasied figure who fails to provide a "reality constraint" for the projections of either sexed child. There is a strong ambivalence expressed in the theory about the subject's relations to objects as a result. The pathological state identified as masculine—in which the milieu of emotional connection is repudiated as feminine in favor of a masculine identification with an absent ego-ideal—is nevertheless relied on to produce the "strong ego boundary" required of the subject whose object relations these are.

This is because parenting that includes an identification with the child is most at risk of producing the lack of individuation: "It seems likely that from their children's earliest childhood, mothers and women tend to identify more with daughters and to help them to differentiate less ..." Not to identify, while producing the differentiation required, nevertheless leads to a masculine subject who is isolated in his fantasied connections to objects: "On the other hand, a mother tends to identify less with her son, and to push him toward differentiation and the taking on of a male role unsuitable to his age, and undesirable at any age in his relationship to her" (49).

This last rider seems to suggest that the maternal relation remains an exception, in which it is psychically healthy to maintain some lack of differentiation.

Her feminist conclusion is to prescribe a maternity in which ego-strength is given through psychical connection with both parents offered to children of both sexes. The underlying idealism in this model of the maternal function does not differ from Winnicott et al., despite its explicit feminist bent. It still understands the maternal on the model of a container in which subjectivity is grown, an "environment" in which the "object" status of the container is not theoretically challenged. Chodorow's innovation perhaps is to extend the "maternal" as a conceptual ideal for *both* parents; the paternal function as a function of *law*, central to other psychoanalytic accounts and indeed to Freud's, is obscured.

In effect, there is no inherent sexual difference, at the level of the psychical, for this paradigm. And although it idealizes the connective maternal as a model for both sexes, it still assumes the subject/object relation which in fact describes Western *masculinity*, as it does technological rationality. In this way, this "feminist psychoanalysis" repeats the progression pursued in second wave "feminism of equality" generally, toward a sexual indifference that is implicitly masculine. Indeed, the affinity with the liberal politics this implies is expressed in the conclusion that

> satisfactory mothering, which does not reproduce particular psychological problems in boys and girls, comes from a person with a firm sense of self and of her own value, whose care is a freely chosen activity rather than a reflection of a conscious and unconscious sense of inescapable connection to and responsibility for her children. (59)

Despite their deep differences, Chodorow shares with Kristeva's reflections on the Virgin Mary, and Irigaray's on the feminine Divine, a yearning in feminist psychological theory and feminism generally; the search by daughters, theoretical and otherwise, for mother figures. For Kristeva, a woman's maternity brings her in close psychical contact with the figure of her own mother. For Irigaray, the childless woman, too, seeks a feminine "ego-Ideal." But it is also true to say that feminism has not yet provided that figure for women's maternity, although other elements of femininity are sought to be celebrated (for example in the recounting of the life of de Beauvoir herself). This lack of figuration points toward the implicitly gendered account of the formation of the superego, as expressive of a paternal law governing masculine desire.

As Oliver puts it, "[I]n a few passing passages and interviews, without explanation, Kristeva almost whispers that perhaps it was also 'necessary to be a woman to attempt to take up that exorbitant wager of carrying the rational project to the outer borders of the signifying venture of men' " (Kristeva, *Desire in Langauge,* quoted in Oliver 1993, 115) In reference to her own theoretical prose, Kristeva has resisted the temptation to write theory as an "avant-garde literature" (Oliver, 114), arguing instead for a specificity given to psychoanalysis to confront the question of the signifier. The Lacanian phallus, in whose shadow this nascent discourse about discourse languishes, is by definition an oppression, "this untenable place where our species resides, threatened by madness beneath the emptiness of heaven" (*Desire in Langauge,* xi). But in Kristeva's conviction, it is still psychoanalysis, and not philosophy—that is to say, language used in the echo of its own semiotic resonances, not in the repression of all but its "cognitive content"—which would open the pathology of the paternal law to rational critique.

Jacqueline Rose argues, in *On Not Being Able to Sleep,* that one of the burdens the mother is given to bear is the paradox of an unconscious communication where there theoretically can be no communication. Citing Kristeva, she comments:

> Belief in the mother is rooted in our fascinated fear with the impoverishment of language. If language is powerless to situate me for, or speak me to, the other, then I presume—I yearn to believe—that someone somewhere will make up for that impoverishment. Someone, or rather someone female, before there was speech, before it—before the unconscious—spoke, before . . . (2003)

Near the start of her essay, she writes:

> Let us call "maternal" that ambivalent principle that is bound to the species on the one hand, and on the other, stems

> from an identity catastrophe that causes the proper Name to toppable over into the unnameable. It is that catastrophe which we imagine as femininity, non-language or the body. (158)

Rose concludes: "One could then say that, if mothers know anything—to give them back their subjectivity in the matter for a moment—it is the travesty of that projection" (159). The asymmetrical and idealized place given to the mother's subjectivity in the object relations picture means that the mother's contribution must itself therefore be the object of anxious concern, since it is impossible, even while it is being insisted upon. Rose makes an insightful assessment of this tradition through the work of Christopher Bollas.

She argues the failures attributed to "bad mothering" by the work of the Independent School are attributed in Bollas to *empirical* circumstance; for example, to "an actual family setting with which (the child's ego) cannot cope" or to parents who can't "identify with their child's needs," etc. But Rose points out it is inconsistent with the commitment to the unconscious to refer to an empirical "reality'" completely outside psychical investment. Why has the mother, of all objects, suddenly become a product of an externality, a "fact of the matter"? As she remarks, what one feminism would read as "the ideological prejudice of the whole tradition," Lacanian psychoanalysis "would see a failure to acknowledge the absence at the heart of being, a way of laying at the door of the mother what is irredeemable about human desire" (152).

> Indeed, you could argue that the emphasis on the adequacy and inadequacy of the mother—what she can and should do—has served to make safe or occlude this space: not the space of a necessary lack-in-being in Lacanian terms, but the opposite, a space too full, a space that will become our dream of the mother, but which is in fact a space with no single origin, and for which no one is accountable, where the divisions inside my own mind, and between me and the other, are unclear. (154–55)

This view of the question highlights the relationship between maternity and epistemology; Rose provides a subtle argument that engages the investment in the mother as an investment in knowledge as such, when she writes:

> It seems to me therefore that there are two very different mothers, or fantasies of the mother, at work in Christopher

> Bollas's writing. Mother as fact, the one safe haven of interpretation (the way one was treated as a child); but then mother, or her space, as the vanishing point of all identities, where no form of knowing could ever reach. (156)

Bollas is known for "the unthought known," his postulate of unconscious knowledge that captures the sense of what is unrepresented but nevertheless experienced, thereby necessarily unconscious (for example, the experience of trauma). Within this category might also lie experiences that predate the possibility of symbolized representation, namely, those of the pre-Oedipal child, and the semiotic of Kristeva's schema. But the insight of the "unthought known," Rose argues, also "spells the end of the fantasy that subjects could ever know each other, or be known" precisely because such communication remains unconscious (156).

> Hence my sense that the most immediate feminist response to this tradition, crucial as it is, is too limiting. For if you simply demand that the Winnicottian image of the mother be modified—saved from her total accountability, recognised even more fully than he did in its radical ambivalence—or more simply demand that she be given her own voice (when does a mother get to speak, where are the case studies of women as mothers in the work?), you none the less remain essentially in the same referential frame. *As long as the question remains: what would be a truer representation of the mother, the limits of knowledge as knowledge remain untouched.* (157, my italics)

LABOR RELATIONS

Even in these semiotically attuned psychoanalyses, maternity is imagined as a *property* of the feminine rather than as a *practice* endemic to it. The insights of Kristeva (and Irigaray, too) as to the significance of maternity still locate it within the claustrophobia of the family, where it has been since Freud, and where it continues to be funded by the masculine anxieties of the Lacanians and contemporary object-relations, discussed above.

However, Irigaray visits Marx through the exchange model of kinship and woman as commodity, in her essay *Commodities Amongst Themselves.* And if the sexed body is to be reintroduced into culture—and the paternal to the body—might not the direction come just as plausibly from a concept of labor? Marxist feminism of the seventies made it plain that women's work was unvalued and uncommodified, as the invisible support of the public domain of capital, where labor was exploited as a kind of commodity. Marxist feminists have long observed the theoretical compatibility of capital with the overhaul of patriarchy—capital being quite prepared to exploit all labor, whatever its gender.

Admittedly, Marxism has had its own troubled relationship with feminism—in the pithy words of Judith Allen, there will be no Marxist feminism until there is a "man" question to go with the "woman" question (Allen and Patton 1983, 92–93). But the insight that is intuitively right about Marxist feminist approaches is that the oppression of child rearing comes not only from the psychosocial *role* that the mother plays in developing subjectivity, but the sexual division of labor in caring for it. The psychoanalytic apparatus of the maternal is fascinating but irrelevant from the point of view of the mother, while what looms large in the phenomenology of motherhood is how much *work* it takes to raise a child.

In this sense, pregnancy is discontinuous with caring for a baby and child, and is not a useful paradigm for maternity at all. From when the baby is born, the mother in no way resorts to a "natural instinct," but works long and hard on behalf of her infant's welfare. This hard labor can be experienced by conscientious fathers, too, since care giving appears at least from this perspective not to be gender determined.

The analysis of the maternal as the ground of subjectivity considers mothering as an extension of gestation. But the reality is arguably far different. In pregnancy, the body will exhibit an astonishing capacity of synthesis and organization to bring about the growth of a foetus to term in the womb, and will then engineer its passage into the world. But from then on, the nurturing of the child is an act of agency burdened with the same choices and limits as other human agency: limited resources, conflicting priorities. That maternity is unlike pregnancy, and is not a product of instinct, is clear from the fact of it being possible to *neglect* a baby or child, but not a foetus.

This marks a possible ontological break between nature and culture (supposing this idea is coherent at all) at birth, and not at the "entry into language," as conventional psychoanalytic wisdom has it. It is common to hear argument on the place of the "chora" and other constructions in the scheme of socialization, yet this "prelinguistic" postulate can strike one who interacts with a baby as remarkably artificial. The prelinguistic is just as commonly substituted in discussion for the "discourse of maternity" that would make sense of it. By contrast, Daniel Stern's descriptions of infant-mother interactions stress their social character; the baby is learning about "what it is like to be with someone" by engaging with his mother's gaze and chatter from earliest infancy. That these are social interactions is most clearly understood when, as he describes, there are "mis-steps in the dance," that is, a mother and child who do not always synchronize their stimulation and attention in such a way as to satisfy each other.

Stern notes the fine line between individuality and idiosyncrasy in this relationship. He warns that experts should be wary of intervening too quickly to pathologize the interactions that are, he says, experienced by the mother as "highly personal and individual to her and her baby, exclusively and unsharably so. Creating and performing in a continually improvised and often idiosyncratic social interaction can be a lonely, even alienating process" (1998, 146).

This loneliness and alienation, also testified to in Rich and other feminist writers writing on maternity, and echoed in many women's experience of motherhood in contemporary life, needs to be explored further in terms of a specifically alienated labor, that is, one alienated from its social character, even when its social character is its primary feature. Indeed, the best analogy Stern can find for this labor is creative work: "I suspect that being a primary caregiver is more like being a creative artist than anything else, performing in your own work as you create it: a choreographer-dancer or a composer-musician" (145).

While this analogy is unsatisfying, for reasons that relate to my introductory discussion of the difference between maternal and intellectual labor, and tends to idealize maternity as a form of art (the maternal being commonly either idealized or abjected in psychological accounts of the child's development), it does place a useful emphasis on *collaboration*. The art forms that Stern is drawn to, in outlining his analogy, are music and dance. As such, Stern's analogy observes maternal labor to be *a labor on the social relation.*

If maternity could be understood on the analogy of creative work, it might be in the sense that creative work, too—and some forms of intellectual labor—all reflect a way of laboring that is, in Marx's terms, "unalienated" (and inalienable).

In *Capital,* Marx outlines the mechanism by which the capitalist must take something more from the labor he purchases, if he is to succeed, that is, he must take "surplus-value." "The self-expansion of capital resolves itself into having the disposal of a definite quantity of other people's unpaid labour" (544), as Marx pungently puts it. Unpaid labor is accumulated from production, and is called ironically "productive labor"; that labor which is exerted above and beyond the necessary effort for making the product and selling it, productive of nothing but surplus value and donated to accumulation. By this reasoning, Marx can observe that the poet is not engaged in productive labor.

"Milton writes *Paradise Lost* like a silk worm spinning silk." And if perhaps the poet sells his manuscript to a publisher, he has merely become a merchant in a chain of production.

The concept of labor, which has its specialized maternal meaning, has also in Marxian theory an ontological place, as activity founding an order that necessarily brings together the individual and the social. The political-economic character of labor is preceded in his taxonomy by undifferentiated yet useful activity by which the human specimen produces the means of subsistence. The "mystical character" of the commodity is missing from these "productive activities" since "it is a physiological fact, that they are functions of the human organism . . . ," which is to say, most purely bodily as distinct from social, "and that each such function, whatever may be its nature or form, is essentially the expenditure of human brain, nerves, muscles, &c" (Marx 1996, 82).

The same reasoning causes Marx to reflect (without irony) that "wherever the want of clothing forced them to it, the human race made clothes for thousands of years, without a single man becoming a tailor" (Marx 1996, 52). But "from the moment that men in any way work for one another, their labour assumes a social form" (82). Women working for men, that is, sewing shirts, for example, are not laboring nor are they thereby included in the social realm.

Can Marx's view of labor before it enters into capitalism illuminate maternal, or for that matter intellectual, labor? As his utopian imaginings depict it, labor is always the working out of subjectivity through activity in relation to nature. He writes eloquently of the satisfactions of labor in an ideal social world:

> Supposing that we had produced in a human manner; each of us would in his production have doubly affirmed himself and his fellow men. I would have [1] objectified in my production my individuality and its peculiarity and thus both in my activity enjoyed an individual expression of my life and also in looking at the object have had the individual pleasure of realizing that my personality was objective, visible to the senses and this a power raised beyond all doubt. [2] In your enjoyment or use of my product I would have had the direct enjoyment of realizing that I had both satisfied a human need by my work and also objectified the human essence and therefore fashioned for another human being the object that met his need. [3] I would have been for you the mediator between you and the species and thus been acknowledged and felt by you as a completion of your own

> essence and a necessary part of yourself and have thus realized that I am confirmed both in your thought and in your love. [4] In my expression of my life I would have fashioned your expression of your life, and thus in my own activity have realized my own essence, my human, my communal essence. (from a note often omitted from the *Economic and Philosophical Manuscripts*, but quoted in McLellan 1975, 34)

Such a description is rich in resonance for the practice of *reproduction.* But under capital, the glamor of the commodity concentrates the love felt by the subject for his objects. "There is a definite social relation between men, that assumes, in their eyes, the fantastic form of relation between things," he writes in *Capital* (43). This mirrored fascination is commodity fetishism, which reflects a labor that is of a "peculiar social character" (ibid).

Like Heidegger (1977) admiring the ambiguous aesthetic excess of the thing itself in *The Origin of the Work of Art,* Marx observes the sheen on the material, which contributes to the simple implement or action its aspect of political economy. As noted above, the "physiological" aspect of labor is posited outside the realm of capital, beyond the reach of alienation and profit. No doubt he imagined bearing and raising children to take place in this twilight, if he thought of it at all.

But Marx also notes that continuing production demands also reproduction, for those elements used in the process must be replenished, and funded. These include "the instruments of labor," and surely also the labor itself. There is, thereby, a reproduction that is the business of political economy. The contemporary success of the reproductive technologies highlights this unnatural labor—the political economy of reproduction has not itself stood still, and a many-faceted science transforms maternity into a technological event. But, despite its conceptual origin in *techne,* it is still not thereby a creative act.

AN ONTOLOGY OF THE MATERNAL

Daniel Stern promises to outline a different subjectivity for women after becoming mothers than before; but he doesn't quite make his case in *The Birth of a Mother.* He shows the preparation of relations to others and objects, but maternal psychical structure is not imagined as changed by it. And yet, this is precisely what appears to be affected, when one reads Adrienne Rich. The accounts of motherhood there suggest that subjectivity is compromised by the demand of another subject whose needs dictate her own space for reflection—her journal entries attest to her struggle to be a poet at the same time as a mother, and to the rage this contest brings out (1998, 21).

However, even what Stern does say in *The Birth of a Mother* attests to the reality that, as a subject, a mother thinks differently. The maternal relation is not the separating out of the subject in her subjectivity from her objects and others, so much as, in her child, the *production* of another not as an object, who is not readily objectifiable. It is the production of a style of embodiment that is nevertheless a social milieu; in its very bodily expression also a kind of labor. Therefore, the maternal suggests a different ontology, a logic not preoccupied by the habit of distinction, and a logic not riven by the law of the excluded middle. A way of thinking of being, which does not separate a subject from its objects, but rather tolerates various differentiation.

Relating the problem of maternity to the problem of the subject and its objects, can bring into focus the subject/object distinction that informs a dominant conception of thought itself. From this perspective, it would appear the maternal can provide not only an ethical but a logical example.

But what does this presage for the intellectual labor that is *ontology*, the theorizing of being, the practice of philosophy? Since mother theory would allow a different ontology for the maternal body, it would also imply an ontology specific to every different body, which is in itself a very different conception of philosophy. Perhaps maternity is not merely incompatible with theory, but puts the existing practice of philosophy, as a generalization and an abstraction, into question. A maternal ontology might show up the specificity of theoretical life, and challenge its claim to universality, just as other explorations of sexual difference have challenged other philosophical claims to the universal. The maternal is an important issue for philosophy, at least for this possibility.

Two questions arise from these reflections on the ontology of the maternal, questions that move in contrary motion, out of the subject/object distinction, and from the observation of this as the technological mode of thought. What follows for thinking and thought from the relaxation of the distinction? And, what happens to the philosophical character of maternity, to an ontology identified above, when reproductive technology commodifies it?

A kind of thought freed from the "copula" of subject and predicate is already imagined in the work of Deleuze (as a thought without image), of Kristeva in the semiotic, of Irigaray in the ethic of sexual specificity, and arguably as early as in Nietzsche, with the formation of self as a work of art. It gives rise to heterogeneous rhetorics that can open philosophy up to the logic of dreams and rhythms. Arguably, it is also a possibility presaged in the cyborg, as contemporary feminists aspire to it, or at least in the excesses of technological innovation.

Meanwhile, a kind of maternity disciplined as a commodity and inducted into the capitalist-democratic mode, may result in more recognition of maternal labor divided between child care centers, nannies, and paid maternity and paternity leave. However, this may merely admit maternity to the dubious register of exploitation by capital, if it cannot also be opened to the technological as itself an ontological event.

It is because *techne* is ontological (to invoke Heidegger) that the advent of a way of thinking is also the becoming of a way of being. We are directed to the significance of thinking maternity, *the necessity of a maternal ontology*, however unimaginable, to meet the risks of these contrary moments.

TWO

Brave New World

What responsibility is given to us in the wake of the future? The challenges presented by the development of reproductive technologies provide a way to dramatize this "thought of new being." The problem is broadly thought of as "ethical"—but are we so sure we understand on what the ethical is predicated? The idea of *responsibility* for events over which we have only limited control, and indeed for which the effects are multiple and unpredictable, is anathema to our technological thinking. In that scheme, the foresight of prognosis would guarantee the place of a governing rationality over the unruly elements of disorder. Yet the future is a challenge to that ordering, and one that is challenged by the changes wrought through, among other things, the reproductive technologies.

News reports seem to appear weekly, noting startling developments in reproductive technologies, developments that seem to conjure the proverbial "Brave New World." In one future, for example, children might be born of unborn biological mothers. In another future, hermaphrodites might "develop normally," and babies could be born with four genetic parents, not two.

There is a striking narrative similarity in these reports, which is characteristic of the reportage of these scientific events currently. In each case, the "breakthrough"—which has been reported to a special interest audience such as a medical conference or journal, rather than directly into the public domain—attracts an inside page report, providing a context for, rather than an event in, daily life. It briefly describes the research in terms of the sex distinctions used in the human social world, for instance, a "she-male" embryo, an "unborn mother." A basic literacy about reproductive science is attributed to the lay reader in the use of terms such as embryos, egg harvesting, female hormones, genetic disorders, immature egg follicles, and the like.

The scientists responsible describe their motivations in terms of a benign quest to help certain categories of afflicted patients of the future, for example, "foetal eggs could be donated to infertile women," or "a new way to cure genetic disorders" might be found. But the ethical commentators all react in the language of outrage: "mind-boggling," "beyond comprehension," "horrific," asking "whether the boundaries of IVF science have finally been pushed too far" or whether the science is "running out of control," and advising that such developments "should remain in the realm of science fiction."

Whose version of the future is correct—the scientists' "could" or the ethicists' "should"? And who is to take responsibility for a future, so changed as to be "mind-boggling" and "beyond comprehension"? Desire for the future is evidenced in the technological drive to reproduce differently as it is emerging in reproductive science. Meanwhile, a horror of the future is evinced in bioethics discourses on that science.

The horror-futures presented in the news reports raise anxiety by threatening us with a disordered future. Take the examples above; in the case of the hermaphrodite, a future is depicted in which gender is disordered; in the case of the child born of the unborn or of many parents, a disordered genealogy.

The hermaphrodite is assumed to horrify, since it crosses the distinction between the sexes on the body itself. This body is abjected by an anxiety related to that which urgently attributes a gender to babies born with expressed ambiguity. But the hermaphrodite is not merely deformed, in the way that other kinds of malformation of the body provoke our narcissistic anxiety. The hermaphrodite *deforms* sexual difference, and is thereby uncanny, too.

Of course, transgendering is already a cultural reality without the science fiction of the "born" hermaphrodite. The "sex reassignment" already accomplishes the transition from one sex to another through the technologies of surgery and hormone therapy. Would the production of this "hermaphrodite" by genetic means render the category of "trannie" more natural—or more technological? Would it create the freedom for some to celebrate their ambivalence, or would it put up another obstacle to the expression of others' experience of sexuality, as for example the feeling of "wanting to *be* a woman"?

The child of many parents disturbs these reports differently from the child with a different morphology. This child "passes" for "one of us." It is their origin which is disordered, a narrative they will give differently. The child born of an unborn mother would feel their difference at the level of identity, an identity that is expressed for others in their knowledge of our relations.

This science fantasy is already represented today in adopted children and the children of gamete donors produced through IVF, both of whom are persuaded of the desire to "find their birth mother/biological father." It highlights Marilyn Strathern's analysis that kinship in Western society is *understood as a biological relationship*, a relationship produced by biology between people who may never have met and thereby have had no other "relation." This is true of everyone's genealogy, when it refers to, for example, great-grandparents who have never been alive in our lifetime. But the attribution of intimacy and identity simply through knowledge of biological similarity seems striking and even odd, when put alongside other expectations of kin, such as love, care, and involvement in each other's lives. As the proverbs run, "It is a wise child who knows its father"; yet, "Blood is thicker than water."

As anthropologist Sarah Franklin notes, the uncovering of kin as an epistemological relation dictated by biological "facts" amounts to the discovery that *kinship is biology* in our society. It isn't so in all societies. "[N]ot everyone assumes people reproduce like animals . . . the importance of modern biological science in shaping understandings of kin relatedness is culturally specific, of recent origin, and uniquely dominant in the Anglo-American context" (2001, 305). Certainly, the ease with which assisted reproduction can be accomplished by the donation of bodily elements (sperm and egg) puts pressure on the significance of this conviction for us.

"According to this definition of kinship, a kinship tie not known to exist can be discovered." Franklin notes that Strathern and others have argued that knowledge and paternity are both, in different ways, *property* relations, and their collusion constitutes an old circularity:

> As Strathern points out, the model of knowledge necessary for the discovery of scientific facts to tell us who we really are also depends on specific, co-dependent concepts of individuality, property and possession. The isomorphism between the way we are seen to possess identities and to possess knowledge of them can be generalized to reveal the way possession of knowledge about the world is so

deeply ingrained in western assumptions about individual agency, identity and subjectivity. (307)

Perhaps the most familiar aspect of the horror show is that of "foetal research." When rumors of the production of a human clone surface, they prompt arguments from ethicists that often dwell on the "unnatural" aspects of such conception, contrasted with present social relations. For example, one bioethicist has described clones as "orphans," for lack of "old-style" genetic descent, and as "laboratory rats," that is, reproduced not with love but with science—thus assuming the two, affect and rationality, to be opposed (Australian Broadcasting Corporation TV "Catalyst" report, 22 Nov. 2001).

Other criticisms continue this theme, of the technological as anathema to the sexual, suggesting that clones are mere "xeroxes" (ignoring the natural occurrence of multiple births) and that this science poses a threat "to the family." The arguments include the ingenious fear that a child may have an "ethical repugnance" at their own conception, a suggestion loaded with pathos. It conjures the threat of being an "unwanted child," comparing the child of technology with the violence of the traditional reproductive order, where children can be conceived as a result of rape.

Perhaps the opposition of the technological to the sexual order is based in part on a familiarity with the workings of instrumental rationality. The foetal stem cells being used for drug testing are potentially lives in themselves; the problem presented by therapeutic cloning for "spare parts" is the problem of means-ends thinking, the fear that the human itself will become the standing reserve of these rational purposes. The sexual order in the discussion of foetal research takes the burden of producing our subjective uniqueness, the "soul" in every body. This is of course deeply paradoxical, given that the concept of the sexual order is at the same time reliant on a postulating of a "natural biology" of sexual reproduction, which is to say a science that is just as firmly designed around instrumental rationality.

In contrast with the ethicists' horror, there has been another common media response to the cloning claims, epitomized in a *Sixty Minutes* report: "It was always going to happen." The presumption that somehow the momentum of technology exceeds the regulation of bioethics is powerfully present in the social understanding of it, and even lends to the ethical outrage the appearance of an ineffectual bluster. As Franklin reports, reviewing a study undertaken by the Wellcome Trust Medicine and Society program into public perceptions of cloning, "the resulting picture emerging . . . was . . . of increasing public suspicion towards scientists, who were seen to be an uncontrolled elite wielding considerable power, which might or might not be used in the interest of the public good, or 'society,' and could not realistically be prevented from going 'out of control' " (*Culturing Biology*, Web version, 5).

The problem for a bioethics that accepts that its normative status *supervenes* on the scientific fact, is that it thereby concedes that it has no authority over the real which is the province of this fact. This is why it may appear lame and as though fighting a rearguard action in relation to the "progress" of the biotechnologies. Its perception that its judgments can influence, not the content of the technological "discoveries" but only the extent to which such paths are gone down, arises from the axiom of objectivity in science. Ethics, as quintessentially an evaluative and judgmental sphere, cannot have that first-order relation to the objective that it imagines constitutes the science it supervises.

But bioethics relies, just as much as the science it criticizes, on the ideal of instrumental rationality. Indeed, the regulation of the social, the productive, and the scientific are brought together through the most general commitment of modernity, as scholars since Weber have explored. In particular, the technological as a form of rationality emerges in the scientific domain well before its philosophical apologists.

There is therefore *an internal logic* linking the task of bioethics—regulation—and its failure in advance to control what it surveys. Its respect for an independent fact of the matter, upon which its judgment can be advanced only literally "after the fact," produces its unwitting skepticism about its own thinking. This problem haunts bioethical positions commonly from the "analytic" side of philosophy, which uphold a view of scientific knowledge built on the distinction of fact from value, in order to be accepted into the scientific discussion.

Bolder critiques, which are generated from a more "postmodern" understanding of science, abandon ideological loyalty to scientific authority. Writes Franklin (ibid): "Whereas bioethics often asks directly if something is right or wrong, and how we know, interpretative social scientific disciplines such as anthropology ask instead how things mean, how knowledge is constructed, and how understandings are produced" (2). Making these interpretations empowers their critiques, but at the risk of sacrificing their supposed scientific propriety, and maybe, too, losing their popular audience.

Of course, instrumentality is also a part of the discourse of the social sciences; the notion of "interpretation" can just as thoroughly produce an "ethical" slant to the writing. In particular, if the analysis of this interpretation goes forward without posing the question of *the subject for whom this meaning or knowledge makes sense*, such analyses still presume that a rational subject can be generalized, and that specific embodiment is not constitutive of his knowledge.

In "A Genethics that makes sense" (Diprose & Ferrell 1991), Rosalyn Diprose explores the concept of ethics that can make this assumption about knowledge, and examines its effects in the forming of genetic theory and practice.

> Despite this distancing and despite a privilege given to an ethics based on universal rational principles, the increasing public scrutiny of the activities of biomedical science suggests a link between science, the specificity of embodiment and ethics. The link is suggestive only. Much of the recent discussion around biomedical ethics does move away from abstract, formal principles, stressing instead individual rights, particular contexts and specific needs. However, the nature of being and individuality is usually assumed in these discussions and rarely is there any analysis of how or why medicine and science, as modes of knowing, are necessarily ethical.

As Diprose argues, while biomedicine does not confess to the constitutive role it may have in the knowledge its theory produces (since such knowledge is "objective scientific fact"), it will acknowledge an influence in matters of its application; this is the role reserved for bioethics in its wake:

> [B]iomedical science claims to "know," at least potentially, the elements and intricate processes which go together to make up a particular body. It also claims to "know" in what ways, and for what reasons, bodies differ. This theoretical mode of biomedical science delineates the source of the specificity of our embodied being—a specificity thought to lie outside that mode of knowing. On the other hand, biomedical practice can alter the texture of the body. Only as this secondary mode of intervention, does biomedical science claim a constitutive role—in its ability to modify human matter.

But,

> [M]edical ethics does not begin with its role in dealing with the "brokenness" of bodies; nor does "genethics" begin with the "misuse" of theory in the practice of effacing differences. Biomedical ethics begins with the formative function of its

> own modes of knowing which, by mapping what remains other to oneself, are complicit with the constitution and dissolution of borders within and between bodies. Our ways of knowing are dependent upon and multiply differences which we then overlook. And in this production and effacement of different habitats we can locate the conditions for the possibility of what is considered "unethical" practice.

Extending the critique in an analysis of surrogacy, Diprose writes of the decision in the "Baby M" case to uphold the contract for surrogacy in the face of the surrogate mother's repudiation of it, that

> forcing a woman to give corporeality through sex or children is unjust, first, because it denies the generosity of women while memorializing that of men. Second, giving involves a metamorphosis, a structuring of a particular situation through incorporation and corporeal reconstitution, the possibility of which is dependent upon the tolerance to it allowed by the lived bodies involved. . . . [I]t seems that while we can consider giving a zygote in a test tube the status of a person and have no problem attaching value to a male gamete, we still render the gifts of women selfless. (58)

OLD TECHNOLOGY

The manifold problems presented to women in performing moral tasks in an ethical universe constituted by instrumentality, are explored in Carol Gilligan's work through a study of the deliberations of several women about whether to have an abortion in the face of an unwanted pregnancy.

In a Different Voice presents this question as a classically moral one for the feminine perspective, since it involves several other people's interests as well as a woman's own, presenting a decision where care might need to be taken. The dilemma impacts on the feminine understanding of the moral sphere directly—it is more direct, and less hypothetical, than the standard ethicists' thought experiment of the violinist who is surgically hooked up to one's body. The dilemma of deciding whether to abort also invariably includes conflict between competing interests—minimally that between woman and foetus. A woman would not consider an abortion if not able to contemplate overriding the foetal claim on life in favor of other considerations. Thus, abortion has within it a conflict that compromises any ethic of care, a situation in which the ethic is both engaged and, at the same time, challenged.

But given that the foetus is not a being with the power of representation, the more apparent conflicts at the point of impact of the decision may well be those growing out of religious and familial dictates, relations with men, and in particular with the father of the foetus, who may have definite views on whether this child should be born. The competing interests of a woman's own personal aspirations may be spoiled, too, and will certainly be modified, by having the child.

The outcome is weighted socially in favor of having the child, because of the nature of woman's role and the expectation of her sacrificing her own interests. But as Gilligan points out, altruism is always compromised in the decision, even if what the woman sacrifices is her own desire to *have* a child, and fulfil her role, in favor of the father or the family's reluctance. However one looks at the "right to life" rhetoric, her conflict is not solved by defining the foetus as *not* a life, for this is as artificial as declaring it to be one. A woman does not get to feel satisfied in her sense of herself where, subscribing to an ethic of care, she decides to abort, for the conflict lies at the crux of the distinction between mother and child, that is, of a distinction forced upon this ambivalent form of life, insisting that each take the other as object for its subjecthood.

By Gilligan's analysis, abortion represents the heart of a paradox for women's moral development, one poised between femininity and adulthood. Performing the feminine role in a moral way is most often to perform a kind of morality belonging to the dependent, the child, or the submissive. Whereas performing the moral task of adulthood within a traditional schema of moral development is more often about autonomy, responsibility, decision making, and action. So whatever else it involves, the decision of abortion involves a confrontation between the demands of femininity and the demands of adulthood. And the more femininity is experienced as an ideal of self-sacrifice, submission, and duty, the harder it becomes to make a decision for oneself in one's own name.

Gilligan gives several examples; decisions to abort made so as to avoid upsetting one's mother; to please the lover; to avoid upsetting his wife—the kinds of decisions that the dominant mode of femininity trains a woman for, as submission to others' needs and authority, but which leave the woman still held responsible for a decision not completely her own. Gilligan does not argue that a woman needs to move from the mores of femininity to those of adulthood in order to make this decision morally—in fact, she argues, she cannot, because these two aspects of her identity are in conflict. The norms of femininity and the norms of adulthood are the difference between the moments of a schema of moral development, representing the dominance of the *masculine* point of view. An ethics of care and the ethics of justice describe the sexual differential in moral thinking, in which a masculine paradigm disguises itself in a universal moral agent. (67)

Abortion most clearly, but several other kinds of reproductive technology, deliver this dilemma to women, because they make a feminine capacity the subject of a *choice*, a paradigm governed by the instrumental. Previously, it was always within the training of submission to accept the conception of a child as fateful, an aura belonging to the whole of reproduction. But with the availability of the medical technology of abortion, that position is increasingly under pressure in a world organised by notions of agency, choice, and the autonomous exercise of the will. To imagine that men are any more able to make this difficult choice morally, or are more exempt from moral dilemma, would be to misunderstand the point—men are not getting off "scot-free." However, the kinds of moral decision that put pressure on the masculine position are of a different kind.

Gilligan argues that there are gender differences to be discerned in views on ethics, both in the popular understanding of the notion of morality, and in the academic analysis of "moral development." She utilizes a thought experiment: Should one commit a wrong to avoid a greater wrong? This is apparently a utilitarian problem, yet it is not always approached like this by girls. For example, in answer a boy might ask, "Would it be fair?," employing an implicit notion of the social contract that proposes fairness as a form of exchange between autonomous equals. However, a girl often gives a different kind of answer, one that does not talk about rights or leaving people free to live their own lives, so much as of taking care of people and taking responsibility for them.

Interestingly, the theoretical understanding of the experiment, in terms of what can be deduced from the differing responses of boys and girls, is also often understood from the presumption of the utilitarian. This leads Gilligan to question whether *morality* is being adequately conceptualized when it is described in the universal mode, or whether what it is really describing is a "masculine" instrumental ethic.

Gilligan highlights the formulation of moral development in psychology as a process much more in keeping with men's understanding of morality than women's. "Moral development," according to that account, employs the three stages of "preconventional," "conventional," and "postconventional," but Gilligan disputes whether the principles that come to govern reflection in the postconventional stage are the same for men and women. She concludes that if one measured women's responses according to the universal moralism, it would be found that women had not attained moral development. But if one interprets their responses as using an ethic of care rather than one of justice, one would see that women had attained a style of postconventional reflection.

Thus, she concludes that, as an abstract task, morality is understood differently by men and women. Men interpret moral behavior as a question primarily of "noninterference" with the freedoms and rights of others—an ethics of justice. But the logic of equality and reciprocity if used to interpret the moral statements of women will result in a denigration of the moral development in the feminine, since women interpret morality more as showing responsibility for others' welfare—an ethics of care.

Given that the definitions are differently gendered, but the academic definitions accorded to morality concur with the masculine perspective, and not with the feminine, a sexed specificity is not being acknowleged in the experience or in the literature. That would generate two kinds of challenge for feminist studies: Feminist action, in seeking to change certain assumptions about how to live, needs to challenge the way such assumptions have been described as universal but are in fact masculine. Further, feminist theory must challenge the way that *action* has been theorized—presented as an objective description, but in fact following a masculine orientation.

Using these established criteria, Gilligan illustrates how a woman's moral sense might commonly develop toward its own "ideal" without conforming to the progression assumed for moral independence in adults, but in reality modeled for men. This alternative morality can also be mobilized by both genders in relation to certain moral objects: the environment, for example, tends to attract an ethics of care, since justice is not usually accorded across the species. Where that debate turns to resources and their distribution, it returns to the ethic of justice. The two, despite occurring together, are not automatically compatible; the ethic of justice recommends a value of independence, while the ethic of care recommends a value of interdependence (105).

The "different voice" of Gilligan's title is more than an eloquent figure. It gestures toward the grammar of a coupling, in which neither the active nor the passive voice would govern their objects but in which *something else might be assembled.* That is to say, it may call for a different relation than that of subject to object for the comprehension of some *ethoi.* Like the earlier discussion of a maternal ontology that may inhabit a world differently, revealing a masculine morality that differs from a feminine morality highlights the *specificity* of ethics, and raises the possibility of a moral development based on yet other principles. It will be argued in later chapters that these differences may be occluded in a technological era in which purposes are governed by instrumental rationality. As such, from within the present "morality" there may be ethics we find difficult to respect, or even to recognize.

CULTURAL TECHNOLOGIES OF REPRODUCTION

Recent research suggests that women may be now confronted with the irony that they must choose to be mothers against the odds, where before they had no choice but to be.

A recent study, *What, No Baby?* (Cannold 2005), finds that more than one-half of its sample could be classified as "thwarted mothers," women for whom the circumstances surrounding the "choice" to be mothers may in effect leave them childless at menopause. This study calls into question the assumptions of several other studies in the area of childlessness that describe these women's position as "childless by choice." Cannold argues that some circumstances can become so constraining in this regard as to be called "chosen" only on the most optimistic analysis. Elements contributing to the optimism include a feminist desire to represent women's control over fertility as valuable in individual women's lives.

These circumstances include: the availability of contraception and the expectation that one will use it, therefore the likelihood of partnerships in the early childbearing years being set up for romance rather than parenting; the availability of abortion, meaning that each pregnancy needs to be chosen rather than becoming something inevitable; the expectation that women will continue in the workforce and even have a "career," which makes the timing of motherhood problematic and tends to defer it, sometimes until the woman is in her late thirties; tolerance in the community of the declining birth rate, meaning that measures to produce less conflict for working parents, better childcare, and more realistic expectations of mothers, and financial relief for families, have not been adequate to the daunting "opportunity cost" of raising children.

Among her most startling suggestions is Cannold's finding that for many women in her study motherhood had come to be regarded as an "irrational" choice. Nevertheless, many of the women still desired to be mothers in the face of the disadvantages—this they tended to attribute to a "maternal drive," a kind of biological imperative that outweighed rational judgment (perhaps like love?).

The concept of the biological was similarly invoked to track the distress that childlessness caused many women, as they approached the age of menopause without having had a child. This was distilled in the phrase "the biological clock," a notion that dominated women's thinking about their reproductive futures except in the case of the actively "childless by choice" subject—a woman who has sought out partnerships and circumstances that would inhibit motherhood from becoming an issue.

But the study analyzes the "biological clock" as being triggered, not by physiological events but by social ones, throwing the distinction it needs to make between the biological and the intentional into doubt. For example, a woman was not likely to "feel" any less fertile at forty than at thirty, but rather was familiar with the general knowledge of declining fertility rates at that age. Similarly, it was not an assessment of her own individual body that governed this panic, but a piece of common knowledge that set the clock to "go off" at forty. Sadly, this led some women to discover their infertility only in the process of exercising their "eleventh hour" option.

The study found a woman's "biological clock" was triggered most often by social circumstances, such as her peers beginning to have children or her family beginning to pressure her, as well as by an introspection brought on about her values regarding work and love after some experience of both. The conclusion that the biological clock is not a biological given, but what we may better call a *functional fantasy* in a system of social representations about the lives of women, is one of several curious paradoxes we are faced with when we consider the radical change to reproductive futures that are before women now.

It may not always be evident that an instrumental rationality must, by its own logic, be driven by purposes and ends. Ironically, then, while presenting itself as the objective and rational form of knowledge, the instrumental by its very design, must be motivated and organized around a desire. Desire seems to be an unavoidable corollary of means and ends, since this teleology comes invested with a certain momentum from one to the other.

Some desires for technology are considered perfectly "normal," even reasonable. The desire of the childless for children of their own makes sense to us, as does the desire of the terminally ill for a cure. The desire for a "better" future promised by technological advance ignites the passions of consumers of all types. In this context, the means of foetal research might appear to justify the ends.

In other recent reportage of the future—the twenty-fifth birthday of the first child born by in vitro fertilization and the death of the first animal clone—desire for children and furry farmyard animals eclipses the horror. Louise celebrates birthdays and Dolly receives an obituary. As *Nature.com* put it, "Celebrity clone dies of drug overdose" (22 August 2003). So the "technological products," Louise and Dolly, become inducted into existing understandings of kinship and gender roles. Naturally, they become part of the scene, including the desire to be like everyone else. Louise says, "My life is pretty normal. There are just special events like this." And Dolly is put with Welsh ram David, producing two lambs the ordinary way. By the time of Louise's twenty-fifth birthday there have been more than a million children born in the world using IVF. The future is becoming present. And if reproduction is about finding the old in the new, we can witness it in the way these technologies adapt, as they adapt themselves to, "traditional family life."

But the point of the reproductive technologies would seem to be *not* to assist nature "to do what she cannot do for herself," but instead to instruct us in desires that are *impossible* in nature. In this way, reproductive technologies play their part in the political imaginary, and generally in "biopower," by cultivating the technological way of thinking in relation to reproduction, which has hitherto been its contrast. The technological versus the sexual is a particular example of the opposition of the cultural and the natural, and indeed the possibility of a *reproductive technology* signals its collapse.

While "technological creep" into the cultural order is accepted, what we may call the "creep" engendered by cultural change is often strenuously resisted. Take the case of gay marriage, recently denounced by the pope. Gay marriage is commonly rejected out of concern for the institution of marriage, which is understood as a bedrock institution of society concerned with reproduction of the family. Like resistance to single women's access to IVF, and to voluntary euthanasia, this view is evidence of sincere conservatism resisting the overturning of the fateful (sexual) by the technological (rational). In this worldview, the social is tied to the sexual is tied to the biological is tied to the evolutionary. As such, it sets itself against technological rationality.

Legislation in several jurisdictions now enables same-sex couples to register their relationships, adopt their partner's children and have access to their partner's superannuation, inheritances, and medical authority rights; this signals the direction of "technological" change. Such social engineering Jefferey Weeks has outlined as a politics of sexual citizenship; those "everyday experiments in living"—from IVF families to gay marriages—which, while lacking legitimacy and formal acceptance, have become increasingly comfortable to inhabit (1981, 1985).

Today he notes that sexual diversity is better tolerated, but still difficult to give full recognition to, and the situation of children in these arrangements is particularly sensitive. But the churches and political parties no longer have a choice about addressing these arrangements—how to live with sexual diversity is a key political issue. The new legislation would seem to propel us toward a utopian future of "full sexual/intimate citizenship." Weeks describes the profound shifts that have occurred in sexual citizenship in half a generation, amounting to a new mutable relation between sexuality and society. Sexuality now matters to society; in the manner outlined in the legislation, it can form the basis of a claim to reproductive rights. And, society matters to sexuality, which is no longer only thought of as a hard-wired instinct, but instead is viewed as highly malleable via prohibition and opportunity.

Foucault's studies of the production of sexuality and/as identity underpin the work of Weeks, Butler, and other "queer theorists." The panopticon is his famous example, a technology for the production of subjects through their experience of desires and fears. This "technology without tools" is another critical conception for understanding both reproduction and the future, since the mode of operation rarely begins with the visible instruments of science. Before the future can be engendered instrumentally, the *desire for it to be assisted*, the desire to reproduce something not produced before, must be engendered.

The desire for political change might be seen as a desire to engender new futures. Feminism has functioned as a crucial political technology, toward the end of changing the institution of patriarchy. For some conservatives, this is tantamount to messing it up: commentators lament the "metrosexual man," for example, and even blame feminism for him. But the headlines might just as well read: "Stop tampering with the future," since the accusation is that political change as an ambition is already a kind of eugenics, an opposing of "history" to nature and to fate. We can see in this the contour of an old issue between conservative and radical politics.

While the theoretical possibility of eugenics appears extreme, and its historical occurrence has been deadly, nevertheless one could argue that "eugenics" is the very principle of reproduction—the logical extension of technologies, traditional and modern, for reproducing a social world by producing subjects in its image. Reproduction as eugenics is an attempt to capture the future. It is an attempt that will necessarily fail; not because it is impossible to practice eugenics (the technology may allow it), but because the future is by definition beyond our reach, as that which is *yet to be determined.*

In this light, feminism no less than conservatism, as political technologies, needs to scrutinize the direction in which they fail. An argument recently put by Derrida, in dialogue with Elizabeth Roudinesco, highlights this failure where he notes that same-sex families are only a particular case of a number of mutations in the notion of the family—"I'm not sure it's the most profound or the most transgressive" (Derrida and Roudinesco 2004, 34). The assumption of the *irreplaceability of the mother* is, Derrida suggests, more challenging to the present culture of the "family"; it would be important to imagine the family that has, not only two or three mothers or two or three fathers, but families with "3 + *n* parents," where parent is not proscribed by gender at all (37).

THE IMPOSSIBLE RESPONSIBILITY OF REPRODUCTION

Franklin:

> [I]t is a mistake to think that we can somehow factor out the hype, the media or the work of the imagination to exaggerate either the promises or the risks of new technology. *This is not going to be possible, now or in the future, because it is precisely the importance of imagining a future yet-to-be which fundamentally defines the whole issue of the new genetics and society.* (*Culturing Biology,* Web version, 10)

Heidegger:

> Today we are too easily inclined either to understand being responsible and being indebted moralistically as a lapse, or else to construe them in terms of effecting. In either case we bar from ourselves the way to the primal meaning of that which is later called causality. . . . The four ways of being responsible bring something into appearance. They let it come forth into presencing. They set it free to that place and so start it on its way, namely, into its complete arrival. The principal characteristic of being responsible is this starting something on its way into arrival. (1977, 316)

The act of responsibility is seen in conventional bioethics as an act of an agent. This agent is itself the technological self, the epitome of the subject distinguished from, and able thereby to take command of, its objects. While it is held in place as a subject by its projection onto others as objects, this subject is nevertheless postulated as freed from these objects, and free of demonic projections that would disturb the "objectivity" of this subject's command. This posture is impossible, despite being demanded of us all.

If responsibility is integral to the distinction of subject/object, and to the means/ends of distinction as such, then it is impossible in the sense Derrida speaks of as aporetic. Derrida speaks specifically of the *experience* of aporia, this unassumable posture of "pulling onself up by one's own bootstraps." The unassumable responsibility of the future can be understood as the responsibility *to experience it as aporetic,* that is, as exceeding our knowledge and our mastery of self and others (cf. *Aporias,* "Gift of Death").

Derrida also proposes an alternative, just as impossible (in a reading of Levinas) in the *Gift of Death.* If responsibility is postulated as the taking on of a venture beyond knowledge and mastery—if responsibility and *faith* go together, as they do in Levinas's thinking—then the impossible responsibility of the future is nevertheless *our* critical venture, *our* critical risk and responsibility. In these two senses, the future presents us with responsibility; unassumable, since we are not that subject of our own scientific fictions; unassumable in the other sense that we are only to be held responsible for that which is beyond our control.

These analyses of responsibility are commonly made "in the shadow of death," in response to the problematic of mortality and the crimes of the past. But Derrida glances occasionally toward the future; at a generation not yet born, as possible subjects toward whom one may owe justice, and toward whom one may have some responsibility. And, more intensely, one could ask: What of the generation destined not to be present because never-to-be-born, or of those whose being hangs on our taking the risks of transformation?

This is the aporia of responsibility for the future. The future and reproduction are *recto* and *verso,* engendering the same impossibility, that of causing what we do not control. While Derrida emphasises the disjunction between the living present and other times, the notion of a genealogy emphasizes just as thoroughly the continuity with the living present. Or perhaps, rather, it highlights the *contiguity* of the present with its past and future, however unrelated they may seem, and however they might be known or remain unfathomable.

THREE

Reproducing Technology

Although today the number of children born with the assistance of reproductive technology is still tiny compared to the vast majority of the population conceived by sexual means, nevertheless its existence flags an important change in embodiment.

Some feminists approach the reproductive technologies on the assumption that democratic tools can critique them. I mean by this that they refer the "safeguards" against technological innovations to one or more of the democratic means; conversation, openness, and accountability; equal representation, stakeholder consultation, antidiscrimination law, and consumer choice. These all are part of the repertoire of good government in the liberal democratic nation-state.

But I am concerned that this approach may be unequal to the task. An examination of the history of nineteenth and twentieth-century thought suggests that democracy and technology arise *together*, both indebted to a means and ends style of thought that is characteristic of modernity. It might be expected that certain realities and futures produced by those technologies will be invisible to its critiques.

Further, the political demands of feminism as well as the techniques of assisted reproduction arise in the context of a gendered world reconfiguring itself. Kinship is reordered and with it, the sexual relation. The paternal metaphor is slowly relinquished in favor of the liberal individual, hierarchy apparently giving way to the democratic and even the "rhizomatic." In this context, the "equalizing" of the sexes is more than a political project—it may be a historical inevitability. But this brings both the problem of sexual difference and its impending "solution" (i.e., its erasure) into view.

What will remain in postmodernity—a future in which the reproductive technologies increasingly feature—of the incalculable sexual difference of a species which until now has been "sexually dimorphic"? And how much—or how little—will it matter that being human has traditionally meant belonging to a series that is reproduced sexually?

THE MODERN

The consequences of the reproductive technologies for the idea of the family are tied to how the ability to manipulate human reproduction might change our social world and the relation between the sexes.

In *Gender and History*, Linda Nicholson argues that by the nineteenth century "kinship systems which at one time had been the major mechanisms for regulating food production and distribution, sexuality, crime and punishment etc were replaced by the twin and separate institutions of the family and state" (1986, 2). The recent changes in the institution of the family allow it to be seen "as a contingent, primarily modern, social institution, in complicated interrelation with other modern social institutions" (1). And she argues that, while feminism is itself a manifestation of changes in the relation of private and public, it also provides us with a vantage point from which to understand these changes (4).

The advent of the reproductive technologies has the potential to change the norms by which society reproduces itself. The deployment of these technologies has the capacity to bring about significant changes in our concepts of "sexual relation"; that is, in concepts of femininity and masculinity, of maternity, paternity, marriage, and the life of the family. But of course, societies, through structures of kinship, have always maintained "technologies" for the reproduction of a culture. The detailed marriage rules of even the most nomadic communities attest to the importance to a social group of the manner through which it permits reproduction (cf. Marilyn Strathern 1992).

To describe these traditional arrangements—from Australian aboriginal moieties to the *Married Women's Property Act*—as technologies acknowledges that technology is not merely a name for machine-based action but any arrangement of resources that allows for the production of a desired end. The patriarchal marriage, for example, has been a ubiquitous means for preserving inheritance not only of literal wealth but of relations between classes of men. This "reproduction" reproduces the social structure at the same time as it reproduces the family line.

To describe reproduction as an opening for technology is also to take up Heidegger's insight that technology, before it is a concrete event, is a "way of thinking." In the *Essay Concerning Technology* (1953), Heidegger identifies technology as first and foremost a way of thinking that powerfully affects what it surveys, by conceiving of nature as a means to an end, and thus as a "standing reserve." As Heidegger notes, the danger of technology is that it does not discriminate among resources—that it will come to regard even its "thinker," that is, the human, as itself a standing reserve.

Contemporary feminist analyses have already identified this reality in the implementation of IVF, for example: the woman herself, and her motherhood becoming tools of a medical technological development and a material acted on in the process of fertilizing her (Corea 1995). Even those feminist theorists who are positive about the prospects for the assisted reproductive technologies warn against this tendency to reduce women and their fertility to "mother machines" (Hubbard 1990).

At the same time, feminists have looked to developments in these (and other) technologies to free women from their traditional reproductive role, and from the patriarchal family, so as to take up equal positions in society with men. These changes are in fact no longer merely theoretical: they are real for many Western women, who now work outside the home in increasing numbers as their domestic labor is abbreviated by "labor-saving" devices and their reproductive labor is modified by the availability of contraception and abortion.

What effect will these changes have on the utility and viability of marriage, which in reproductive terms has provided membership of a group for each child, under the auspices of a male head and reproducing the conventional understanding of the roles of men and women? Despite technological advances, Kelly Oliver's discussion in *Family Values*, informed by psychoanalytic theory, argues that "the fantasy of the nuclear family is still a centerpiece of our cultural imaginary" (1997, xvii).

And this is undoubtedly a site of visible conflict in relation to the technologies at the present time. For example, debate about just who should have access to publicly funded IVF services, and whether this should include single women and lesbian couples, draws heavily on anxiety-nostalgia for a childhood under the protection of "a mummy and a daddy"—a safety that never quite was.

Discussion of the reproductive technologies in feminist ethics is commonly pursued around questions of the value of the technology to women's aspirations. Laura Purdy, for example, writes: "The central issue is whether these new techniques are moral and ought to be used" (1996, 171), and answers in the (weak) affirmative. She engages with several antifeminist authors, highlighting the logical flaws in the case for "leaving nature as God intended."

Drucilla Cornell, reflecting on the concepts of freedom and equality in their legal and feminist senses, as they apply in the "emotionally fraught sphere of life we call sex" (1995, 3), approaches the question not through morality but through justice. She argues for a "feminist re-statement of why we should prioritize justice over the good" (27). And against the specter of Orwell's *Brave New World*, Cornell nevertheless explores the domain of the social imaginary, declaring, "Feminism is ultimately about politically taking that chance to create new worlds" (ibid., and cf. Moira Gatens's 1996 discussion of the social imaginary).

Ruth Hubbard's conclusion, in *The Politics of Women's Biology*, represents the predominant "reasonableness" of the feminist position. While warning against the training up of a new breed of experts—the bioethicists—to form yet another barrier to women themselves being heard on the subject of their reproductive lives, and questioning what kind of "choice" the new technologies open up, Hubbard comes back to the importance of democratic safeguards in the progress of this technology. Her argument is not that where the science has been abusive—as in the selective eugenics of Nazi Germany in the thirties—it is a case of "bad" science departing from traditional norms, but rather that science without consciousness of its place in the political landscape is inherently a threat to the interests of the less powerful.

Assisted reproductive technologies may continue to be more or less successfully overseen by democratic processes, at least as far as they are dependent on funding which comes from the wider political scene—the research councils and private philanthropic bodies of the democratic nation-states, or by the fees paid by those desiring it. Feminist thinkers and actors need to enfranchise themselves in this discussion, Hubbard prescribes.

But some feminists, while advocating social justice, question the extent to which these technologies can be rewritten in feminist terms. As Debra Steinberg argues, disentangling IVF from its "eugenic, embryo/logic and recombinant sensibilities" is problematic, since it implies divorcing this sphere of reproductive medicine from conventional discourses of family, and from the historical role of medicine as an agency of sexual and reproductive regulation and control (1997, 194).

THE RECHERCHÉ

The philosophy of technology is "still widely regarded as not much more than a small and not particularly prestigious area of specialization," Scharff and Dusek write, as a result of the assumption made in the Anglo-American "analytic" and European "positivist" traditions that technology is "an unproblematically beneficial force for human progress" (2002, 3).

Historically the distinction appears in Plato and Aristotle between theoretical and practical understanding, and the hierarchy of these kinds of knowledge is there set up. But the ethic of a kind of *human* control of the natural is modern; in Greece, *techne* mimicked the natural world, while in the medieval Christianity that followed, progress toward salvation presaged the modern teleology captured in the thought of human progress.

For Francis Bacon, knowledge was power over nature, which category included women, as Genevieve Lloyd critiques in detail in *Man of Reason*. For Kant, the natural purposes of man *(sic)* as an animal is his "scientific and ethical rationality." The authors note; "Kant's portrayal of rational progress seems to justify the enlightenment doctrines about our elevation above and over against nature" (5). The "priestly" role accorded scientists and technologists originates with Comte.

Marx gives an ambivalent but central place to technology: does technology direct capital/class struggle or does capital/class struggle direct technological progress? At stake is technological versus the social division of labor, to which Engels's "scientific socialism" makes a contribution. Marx also postulates an "evolutionary conception of humans as essentially tool-making animals"; Hannah Arendt criticizes this, observing that "Marx's own concept of labour betrays a deep ambivalence between understanding technological labour, on the one hand, as involving creative world-construction and on the other hand, as inseparably linked to degrading oppression" (7).

Current philosophical investigations of technology often confine themselves to identifying philosophical "issues" that arise in technology and its applications, rather than in asking what counts as technology, or examining the relationship posited between technology and science. In this perspective, technology is assumed to be applied science, betraying, as Scharff and Dusek put it, the "naïve influence" of realism, empiricism, and positivism.

Elsewhere, there are more sophisticated critiques, among them the feminist critique of science, for example in the work of Nancy

Tuana; add the contemporary pragmatist readings made by Rorty and Putnam, of Dewey. Dilthey and Husserl provide the context for Heidegger's own reflections on technology. Bruno Latour writes of the anthropology of the laboratory, thereby "popularizes (often without crediting) Michel Foucault's power-network interpretations of human activities and the deconstructive techniques of Jacques Derrida" (85). From Gaston Bachelard, to Jean-Francois Lyotard and Jean Baudrillard, "the post-Kuhnian, pragmatic, and hermeneutic approaches to science raise questions concerning the relation of Western science to traditional or indigenous science in the non-Western world."

Kristen Shrader-Frechette summarizes the task of philosophy of technology as the ethical evaluation of technological applications. This appears to be the most popular position, presently, on the role of philosophy in the enterprise. "For example, questions of the political and social responsibility of engineers and scientists, as well as risk-benefit analyses of technological projects and systems, are major concerns of policy scientists as well as (especially) analytic philosophers of technology" (171).

But the evaluation will necessarily rely on a preexisting definition of technology as a kind of objectivity. Technology defined in terms of a "philosophical anthropology," as the expression of unique human capacities, is credited to Gehlen. Such accounts are ubiquitous and appear self-evident, yet there are rivals in the "social constructionist" accounts of technology (such as Langdon Winner's) where the reality of results or their objectivity may be bracketed, or even be regarded with outright skepticism (209).

Heidegger's reading of technology is variously interpreted and qualified by Ihde, Borgmann, Dreyfus, and Feenberg, among others. Feenberg, for example, as Scharf and Dusek summarize it

> concludes that Heidegger's critique of technology's dangers—in spite of its insightful identification of technological excess—can only give us the useless advice that we should somehow "liberate" ourselves from technological engagements. The question of whether this interpretation is correct—and whether this makes any difference to the concrete question of how technological engagements might be delimited and transformed—has become a central issue in the debates over the importance of Heidegger's work. (2002, 251)

Contemporary studies into the nature of technology from a more Deleuzian perspective offer a radical conception of the conjoining of matter and form in a monad metaphysics. Of these, *Transductions*, by Adrian Mackenzie, is notable for its adoption of explicit feminist approaches to corporeality to portray his version of events (see also Parisi 2004). Like much Deleuzian-inspired work, the study is itself a technology, complete with a technical vocabulary for deployment on the problem. The galvanizing of metaphor and the recruitment of vision are faithful to their rhetorical inspiration in Deleuze and Guattari's *Anti-Oedipus* and *A Thousand Plateaux*, and to the technoscience rhapsodies of Donna Haraway. The latter are discussed in more detail in my final chapter.

THE POSTMODERN

Debra Steinberg voices a common fear that social justice advocacy has evinced regarding feminism of the "postmodern" variety: "[A]ll too often post-modernism involves a discussion of difference without a discussion of power relations" (1997, 194).

The desire for IVF might be said to be engendered from the power relations that manufacture knowledge, specifically the knowledge that it is natural for women to bear children, and that medicine heals disability (i.e., not bearing children). But feminist knowledge, too, to the extent it produces desire for identities for women other than motherhood, is also (re)produced through power—Steinberg asks; "If eugenic conceptions are integral to the technology, how can women be enabled not to want it?" (ibid.).

Ironically, manipulating women's desire so that we are "enabled not to want it" may sound at least as brave new world to some ears as the reproductive technology it challenges. This highlights feminism as a political reproductive technology, one for reproducing (feminist) subjects. Certain power relations produce feminist knowledge and it may no longer be a case of "escaping" from repressive power relations, but rather of evaluating the chances of intensifying others. The constitution of identities is a power issue that simple appeal to women's experience cannot antidote, since experience itself is a product of those constituting relations (see my discussion in Ferrell 2000). Rebecca Albury (1999) represents vividly the complexities, ambivalence, and nuances in those power relations that, despite being expressed in the plural, more often coagulate in the single noun *power.*

Based as it is in a concept of "adequation," that is, the bringing together in a common plane of different and competing interests, "social justice" is itself part of technological thinking. We can ask even of the politically correct prescription: What kind of world does it reproduce? Its limitations arise from the conceptual paradigm common to democracy and technology: they both analyze their means into units of equivalence capable of exchange. This means that reproduction is conceived of, in the marketplace as well as in the sexual realm, as a matter of generating more of what there is. This is a reproduction understood primarily as repetition and replication; mechanical, foreseeable, and without innovation.

Justice will be a leading concept in this paradigm, just because it proceeds toward adequation—equivalence—in search of a common ground from which to pronounce judgment. Feminism, as a demand for social justice, is well within this circuit of conceptual exchange. But the more it forges an alliance with justice, the less it can calculate its incalculable remainder—the difference that sexual difference makes in engendering the feminine, or indeed, any gendered "other".

In *The Bodies of Women* as elsewhere, Rosalyn Diprose has shown how biomedical interventions in human reproduction tend to highlight weaknesses in conventional ethical theory, in their inability to take bodily and sexual difference into account (1991,1994). And Fox Keller diagnoses a similar disability in the postmodern: "For all the divergences between advocates of the autonomy of language and those of the autonomy of science, one cannot but be struck by their resonances, by their convergent embrace of the very romance of disembodiment" (1992, 180).

Quoting Baudrillard—"From now on signs will exchange among themselves exclusively, without interacting with the real"—she writes:

> If such entities as subjects, motivated by desire and intention, ever did exist, they clearly do no longer; the subject has been vanquished by "the sovereign power of the object." At the other extreme of realist scientific discourse, human subjects are equally invisible, their material, embodied presence equally ephemeral and inconsequential . . . the search of biologists for the building blocks of life leads them into the realm of pure information. . . . The substantive component of the gene is said to lie in its nucleotide sequence, and that can be stored in data banks and transmitted by electronic mail. (179)

Haraway's expansive study in *Modest Witness* (1997) traces an intricate web of cultural and scientific connections through this ideological field (see chapter 9 for further discussion of Haraway).

The faith in sexual equality as a real historical outcome is mirrored in the faith in science that foresees "progress" as its result. Sarah

Franklin's analysis of IVF failure is instructive in this regard. Despite the advancement of biological science and technology, the high fail rate of IVF—only one in five women conceive using it—renders conception "opaque," she argues. IVF failure attests to an ignorance of the facts of life, which can supply a causal explanation only post facto (1997, 200). She makes the point not in order to cast doubt on the efficacy of the technology, but to draw attention to the social iconography surrounding it—the rhetoric of hope for "miracle babies" and faith in science.

That such religious parallels appear in the context of evocative imagery concerning reproduction is hardly surprising given the importance of belief about conception to cultural accounts of human origins or genesis. As anthropologists have been quick to discover elsewhere, beliefs about conception are inseparable from questions about what it is to be human (Franklin 1997, 200).

In pursuing this iconography, Franklin offers an answer to the "haunting" question with which Adele Clark's insightful study of the emergence of reproductive science concludes: "Why did the reproductive sciences receive the extensive and prestigious institutional and financial support they did when they were and remain so deeply illegitimate and controversial?" (274). Drawing on the historical importance of "conceiving" as "both an epistemological and a procreative act" (199), Franklin concludes that "through IVF, science and nature are unified in an act of pro-creation" that affirms the truth effects of science: the "miracle baby" and the "desperate" infertile woman are evidence of "not only a devotion to the ideals of scientific and technological progress, *but their capacity to be embodied*" (207). Thus, "the biological facts of human reproduction not only signify the 'truth' of reproduction, they *signify the power of science to determine this truth*" (208, and cf. Vasseleu 1991 for a related argument concerning medical imaging).

Reproductive science, Clarke argues, from birth control to the human genome project, suffers from an ethic of modernity—the rationalization of nature (1998, 276). Tracing the history of the discipline of reproductive science, she notes that "cloning and genetic manipulation are quite likely to be the most controversial of all reproductive technologies, exceeding in the twenty-first century the controversy surrounding birth control and abortion in the twentieth" (252). Each of the techniques of reproductive science have been held to be illegitimate, in that they are associated either with taboos on sexuality, perceptions of quackery, and/or with engendering "Brave New Worlds." But the last effect is "truly revolutionary," she suggests: "The capacity to create 'brave new worlds' bridges modern and postmodern approaches to reproduction" (253).

Franklin's view goes beyond the observation of a "modernist project of controlling life itself" by rationalizing and industrializing reproductive processes, to a postmodern kinship theory, the "study of vital signs." And in this connection, Judith Butler's influential theorizing of the production of gender, in *Gender Trouble* and *Bodies That Matter,* also opens onto the realm of the postmodern (cf. Butler 1990,1993).

What has had to change in a way of thinking, to allow the reproductive technologies to be deployed in the way they have already been? It is only as a consequence of *political* technologies such as "universal suffrage" and "sexual equality" that these changes to reproduction can be conceived, let alone conceived of as desirable. Ironically, it can be observed that feminism is itself the most significant of these political technologies for intervention in the sphere of sexual relations. (I discuss the notion of a "technology of gender," advanced in the work of Teresa de Lauretis and Donna Haraway, in chapter 9.)

Describing feminisms as technologies connects a concept of technology to one of power, in order to comprehend "re/productive relations." The medical technologies of assisted reproduction and the political technologies of feminism come to be seen as two sides of the same coin, expressive of postmodernity and its concepts of individual and social life. In tracing the common root of technology and democracy in modernity, one might expect that democracy will *protect* both the advancement of the technology, and the aims of the social equivalence on which it is premised. The spinning out of the technological is *the same idea* as the development of the democratic regime. It is, indeed, the enemy within that drives anxiety about this technology, just because it implements a world that is already conceived (of) in the political imaginary.

The rhetoric of "safeguards" against a "brave new world" needs to be qualified by a political discourse that explores the prospects for technologically engendered realms, political and medical. If technology is a way of thinking, then feminism might need to "think with technology against technology," in the interests of a reproduction that can engender the new.

THE THOUGHT OF NEW BEING

The sexual becomes technologized, like other life processes, in an expanding narrative of scientific progress. Already, the plausibility of cloning and other horizons of reproductive technologies expresses the expectation we already have that the sexual, as the fateful, will become a lost order. If Heidegger is right about technology as a way of thinking, and if Foucault is prescient in his vision of biopower as a form of the government of life, then we are "in great danger" (to quote Heidegger) from the reproductive technologies.

Further, we do not have a defense in the rationalities of the human sciences, any more than we do in the resistances of feminist and environmental politics. These too are born of the same oblivion of thought—technology as a way of thinking that puts an end to thinking while it insinuates itself into being. But what does it mean to say we are in "great danger"? Is this an exaggeration, a melodrama? To what danger, specifically, are we exposed?

The answer is, to a transformation. We think we control our means of reproduction with the reproductive technologies; we think we initiate it with our science, direct it with our choices and thus with our desires, regulate it with our government of "checks and balances." In thinking this, we think technologically. When all the time it is an *unthought* that is thinking us—far from reproducing ourselves, or even regenerating, we are transforming ourselves, and even deforming and mutating. Ironically, in the oblivion of the other, we are in danger of becoming *other than* ourselves.

"Bioethics" may regulate reproductive technology in that, since the democratic means is another aspect of the technological, it will safeguard the interests of it. But it has nothing to say to the ontological. "Bioethics" is not thinking, in that sense, and we cannot be satisfied with it as a feminist response.

Instead, we need to think through the body and its resistances; we need to find the thought of the technologized body as well as of the sexualized. It becomes imperative for the thinker to think across the grain, to seek the new thought for this new being. Specifically in relation to reproductive technology, the feminist thinker has a unique burden in the ontological scheme: she needs to seek the unthought, and to give expression to the affects, stifled by the technological means of reproduction, to think the excessive and the other.

But to do this, the feminist thinker needs first to interrogate her own conceptual milieu, to understand feminist thought, and even more importantly, feminist *un*thought. The next chapters, then, offer an exploration of the terms and conditions of feminist theories.

FOUR

Conceiving of Feminism

Feminist theories are founded on an article of faith: the intuition that there is an imbalance between women and men, and that this imbalance is not an innocent one, but instead profits one party over the other. Describing the imbalance as an oppression or as an inequality gives a different inflection to this political intuition. But to the extent that it is a theory of the imbalance, and of discrimination arising for one group on the basis of their distinction from another, then we can say that feminism is a critique or a theory of that relation. Feminism, if it has an object, has as its object the sexual relation.

Feminism also exists in history, making it at least a collection of events with dates attached. A history gives it an epoch and era, in terms of dates: the winning of suffrage, for example, and other key pieces of legislation. Time marks a history of feminism, and in that, its progress or accomplishment. The *success* of feminism warrants the philosophical examination of the different varieties of feminist analyses of society, and of the collection of projects for change that has indeed brought change about.

But from another angle, it has not been easy to pose feminism in the context of the history of ideas, because it has been *too* contemporary, too present; and also because there is an anxiety in some quarters of feminism that to view it in that way will undercut its particular kind of commitment. To identify feminist demands as arising in a history, other than that of its accomplishment, can even be seen as a threatening gesture, as *anti*-feminist. Viewing feminism as a history of ideas creates the kind of anxiety produced for any normative theory, when it is invited to reflect on the process of its own construction, rather than on its judgment, which it takes to be self-evident.

What is lost in bringing philosophical scrutiny to bear on a political commitment? This question is worth asking, with care. There are times and places politically for certain questions to be asked; and the time for scrutiny of feminism, if it has come, has arrived only very recently. And perhaps it has arisen only because of a loss of impetus in the practice; perhaps this is what would justify the question from the feminist point of view.

Feminist theories are normative theories. It does not make sense to think of feminism without a prescription for how a state of affairs—the relation between the sexes—ought to be arranged, or at least how it ought to be judged. As such, these theories fall within the class of political and ethical philosophies. Many are theories of power, and its distribution as it occurs across gender lines, making them political philosophies; and they are also critiques of social relations, therefore broadly ethical.

Feminist theories are also empiricist, by which I mean, *committed to experience as the measure of knowledge.* These theories by definition seek to change something: it makes little sense to imagine a normative theory based on an a priori—if it cannot be changed, how could it be the subject of a liberationist critique? Feminism needs to argue that this imbalance, oppression, inequality, discrimination, is an a posteriori experience in the world that can be modified, or at least, protested. This brings it to an anxiety about essentialism: the distinction between masculine and feminine is of long standing. Were the factors that produce that imbalance to be essential to the relation, then the possibility for change is thought to be expunged.

In her own history of bringing feminism to philosophy, Michèle le Doeuff describes the point in her relation between philosophy and politics, between a philosophical procedure and a political demand, as a clash between analysis and conviction. She writes:

> Thus a phrase concerning every woman's right to choose cannot be absolutely and unanswerably grounded in philosophical arguments. Having seen philosophy and its rigour having been used to undermine a language of demand, despite the efficacy of that language where it was being used, I despaired of the meeting of philosophy and feminism and fled into classical studies on the renaissance so that I could go on being simply a feminist on Saturday afternoon dem-

> onstrations, for example, with no particular theory and without feeling the need for one.

This reflects the common tension within feminism between theory and practice. The notion that le Doeuff resorts to is surprising for a philosopher, the sentiment that one could simply do without theory, as though there were a theory-free space on Saturday afternoons. It does not persist in her philosophical or political practice, but it does stand as a desire in an empiricist mood; empiricist philosophy expresses the same thing when it sees some things as self-evident, and asserts that there need be no argument about the reality of the world around us.

Perhaps empiricism has come naturally to feminism because of the origin of the sense of oppression literally in *sense*, in feeling. When ideology may run in an opposing direction, the feminist woman can refer to her own feeling of there being an injustice. It presents injustice as an immediate intuition, one that can be experienced without the need for theory. It has proved to be possible to galvanize women to the cause of feminism by referring us to our feelings and experience, highlighting feminism as a philosophy of experience.

This philosophy of experience can be explored in a discussion of feminist slogans, as emblematic of feminist commitments, and as illustrative of some of its difficulties. Considering the slogan also brings into focus how feminism has existed as a practice as much as a theory from the beginning. It has been inaugurated in political meetings as much as in the publication of *The Second Sex*, and action has always been the companion of theory.

SLOGANS

"A Woman's Right to Choose" was an important expression of the will to self-determination on the part of feminist women. It immediately directs us to a public discourse about rights, about contract and, thereby, liberalism. It is the fiction of the social contract that instigates the force of the notion of rights. There is a history to that, too—in, for example, the French Revolution; it would make no sense to call on a *woman's* right without the prior discourse of liberalism, which describes the "rights of man." The slogan posits feminism as a discourse consequent upon liberal political philosophy. The connection to liberal political theory is explored in the work, for example, of Moira Gatens and Carole Pateman.

"Feminism of Equality" has been very successful, delivering legal representation of women's changed role, legislative intervention in the sexual sphere, and correcting to some extent the imbalances that the women of "first wave feminism" protested. How can anyone doubt the importance of suffrage? It was the symbol of women having joined, or of having been joined to, the social contract.

The consequences of taking on the ideas of liberalism and its social contract in the ideas of "right" and "choice" is to direct our attention back to what liberalism arose itself to defend. Its object was the liberal individual, this Man, in which woman now participates. The liberal subject, as it has become described, has a number of inalienable rights, and among them is autonomy and the right to self-determination, choice being the exercise of that autonomy and self-control. These remain potent values for us, and even where they crumble at the edges, they have formed us as citizens.

Characteristic of the liberal subject was his equality—"All men are created equal." Theoretically, this amounts to subjects having become units of equivalence for each other in the sight of their social contract under the rule of law. But the consequence of equivalence is equivocal, in relation to a discussion of the sexual relation. There are two kinds of thing in sexual relation, one called man and one woman, and how significant is the difference between them? "Feminisms of Equality" have strived to reduce that difference to greater or less effect, through equal opportunity and affirmative action, and in tackling the arrangements that do seem to make a difference, such as child care and marital property.

But in terms of public life, the notion of equality between subjects has been able to accommodate extension to the case of women as long as the question of what happened in the private domain, from which it previously distinguished itself, was able to be similarly regulated. Hence, functions that once were private—counselling on feelings, conscience, and familial relations—have been brought into public, through the divorce court, the marriage counselor, the abortion clinic, the women's refuge, and the social security department. These are moves with which feminism has been intimately concerned.

As well as the involvement of the public in the private, this slogan of "A Woman's Right to Choose" allies feminism with a certain faith in rationality. It produces the domain of feminism as that of law, legislation, and government; that is, organized by rational principle, as distinct from the affective. Throughout the history of political philosophy, the public sphere has been assumed to be the sphere of reason, as opposed to the passions, as Genevieve Lloyd (1984) has argued. As such, it is also conscious and relates to a kind of consciousness desired of, and in, the public sphere.

As a theory in pursuit of consciousness, feminist practice invented "consciousness-raising." But this inadvertently complicates the public sphere in a daunting way, by raising the specter of a *lack* of consciousness; if consciousness must be raised, then having consciousness of injustices done against one cannot be a natural accompaniment of experiencing them. This raises a difficulty for a simple empirical appeal to feeling and intuition. While the sexual relation might be analyzed as unbalanced and exploitative, it is a ubiquitous experience of women to love men, and frequently to identify themselves, and to be identified—as wives and daughters—through them. If sometimes as women we decide on what we need and what we want from men, against our interests, on wrong priorities, and from lack of consciousness, then in putting forward a truth (sexual subordination), feminism also draws attention to an endemic error.

The political question, then, that consciousness raising puts to liberalism, is where and how this bifurcation develops in the optic of experience and judging it. While calling on the virtues of consciousness, the case of feminism also tends to undermine them. To the extent that in the discovery of truth has been the recognition of error, feminism has never had the possibility of being straightforwardly empiricist. Something in the case of sexual difference conjures a tension between experience and knowledge.

The very success of the call for redress to the imbalance between the sexes, as a call for "women's rights," prompts analysis of feminisms of equality as versions of the success of liberal theory. Its plausibility and coherence reflect not its self-evident truth so much as the force with which it positively forms the contemporary world.

The slogan "The Personal is the Political" can be seen as a response to this bifurcation. "The personal is the political" became important to feminist politics as a way of making visible what was not visible. Whatever the theoretical status of "false consciousness" (a theoretical problem inherited from Marxism), "the personal is the political" allowed the feminist movement to bring into its sphere of examination things that were normally left in the dark, in what was classically the feminine domain associated with the body and feeling. They were those things that it was considered not appropriate to discuss in public life, but that it was necessary to discuss in order to advance the notion of the woman's right. The woman's right qua woman involved a discussion of things that were not traditionally considered the subject of rights at all. In order to make them visible theoretically, this struggle between the domains of public and private, as "the personal and the political," was invoked. In this manner, feminist practice took the empirical paradox it began with, and nurtured it quite truthfully, finding strategies to deal with ambivalence.

Modes of expression such as fiction, biography, and autobiography were used by feminist writers to make public certain private aspects, but also to take seriously the notion of the *personal*, which was not just the private. It allowed feminists to look at the question of the subjectivity of that which had previously been objectified. In that way, women's subjectivity and finding its self-expression became an important part of the political project.

That, too, involved raising consciousness. There was proposed to be a self-forming available in the self-expression, and a psychoanalytic precept of the healing power of consciousness was adopted without hesitation. Consciousness raising gave a possibility of both individual becoming and, through it, of bringing about the social change the movement sought. In raising consciousness in this way, and in doing so through the questions of feeling and the body, a discussion ignited around desire and sexuality. As well as being a relation of oppression for feminism, the sexual relation now also became configured as a pleasurable relation.

"The personal is the political" led more to a notion of the unconscious than to false consciousness, producing the visibility of feeling, and evoking the extrarational dimension. It intersected with discussions on the nature of mind and body, and interestingly, in this manner, brought some feminism explicitly into contact with philosophy, especially "French philosophy." To the extent that it implies a concept of an unconscious, this style of feminism cannot be said to be a straightforward empiricism, even though from another angle "the personal is the political" is clearly an affirmation of the validity of experience in its subjective concerns.

But because it did not take up the question of experience in the same way as liberalism had, let alone British empiricism, logical positivism, and other philosophical derivatives, this feminism was in conflict with standard scientific expectations—and perhaps this could be predicted, in the attempt to make visible something that was not apparently self-evident.

In effect, feminist theory in these two slogans reveals itself to be centrally concerned with the questions that are raised by empiricism. By producing a theoretical tension between spheres (public/private, body/mind, feeling/reason, personal/political, sexual/intellectual, conscious/unconscious), feminism has opened up not only analyses of the predicament it started from but also a critique of other theoretical worlds.

But despite its desire for empiricism, feminist theory nevertheless requires a more sophisticated hermeneutic than classical empiricism has allowed, and it has never, despite academic dismay, been inclined to stay wholly within the rational, the conscious, and the public spheres.

In considering feminism as a theoretical event, then, we might better understand its present dichotomous state. Feminism, which promotes a normativity that it takes to be a conscious virtue, is kin to other political philosophies that care about consciousness, rationality, and justice. In this, it is close to masculine styles of theory which at another level it may need to reject. The problem for feminism of consciousness is that it is a kind of masculinism, and thereby runs the risk of losing the sexual difference that it set out to analyze and protect.

It is juxtaposed to feminist philosophies that are more informed by notions of the unconscious, and which interpret the feminist project as having affinities with that endeavor, to awaken what is repressed. But the correlative problem, for a feminism of the unconscious, is the constant danger of disappearing into the occult side and losing the potential for rational discussion. It faces the difficulty of avoiding the pervasive and oppressive definitions of femininity given in virulent masculine privilege. This feminism is naked in the flame.

MOTHER OF THE BOOK

As a history of ideas, feminism has the beginnings of a tradition, the continuity from "mothers" such as Simone de Beauvoir to "daughters" of second wave feminist writing, discussed above, and the filial relations that cluster around that history. These kinship metaphors are striking in feminist writing about itself; courtships, maternal relations, appeals to sisterhood, and sometimes the assertion of fraternal relations with other struggles (e.g., Marxism).

One of the myths of origin of this history is the publication of *The Second Sex.* So perhaps it is not surprising that Simone de Beauvoir is part of Michèle le Doeuff's imaginary in her "essay concerning women, philosophy etc," *Hipparchia's Choice.* Her book is a kind of consequence of *The Second Sex,* creating the possibility of lineage and of generation, and leading us to the figure of mother and daughter. As "the mother of the book," de Beauvoir is figured as the mother of modern feminism.

> In an interview with an American journalist in 1976, Simone de Beauvoir said that her book influenced only women who

> wanted to be influenced and helped the development of only those women who had already started to develop by themselves . . . she is not doing herself justice. A book which puts an end to loneliness, which teaches people to see, has greater and more immediate importance than all the manifestos in the world. . . . *Simone de Beauvoir taught young women that we were to trust ourselves and to send the ball back—we who were too often surrounded by cruel words and glances quick to censure.* (1991, 57, my italics)

In the protective tone of the phrase "cruel words and glances quick to censure," the pedagogical as a maternal function is expressed. And Le Doeuff notes that, as mother of the movement giving birth to this famous book, de Beauvoir "still manages to highlight issues and put forward thoughts of which the least one can say is that they galvanized women's movements pretty well everywhere and helped them get going" (56). Le Doeuff writes of sensing "in these lines, the ageing of a philosophy," an expression that carries an image of the mother's face within it.

Another figure arises in de Beauvoir's writing of philosophy because of her "marriage" to Sartre (the couple's informality notwithstanding). De Beauvoir created this figure, which could be described as the "author of the bride," through her autobiographical writing, which has produced another textual role model for feminists. More generally, it has governed some interpretations of feminism and philosophy, which figure philosophy as masculine and feminism as feminine, modeling a relation between these two intellectual fields on the metaphor of courtship.

As le Doeuff evokes this figure:

> The ethics underlying Beauvoir's thought are not hard to identify since she says herself that her point of view is that of existentialist morality. *The Second Sex* is also a labour of love, and as a wedding gift she brings a singular confirmation of the validity of Sartrism: your thought makes possible an understanding of women's condition, your philosophy sets me on the road to my emancipation—your truth will make me free. (59)

The book appears here as a wedding gift to a personal messiah—but le Doeuff is not as tender toward Sartre. Her arguments against him are well done (57–88). However, despatching Sartre, le Doeuff also despatches summarily the value of de Beauvoir's own desire for, and loyalty to, him, with the notion of the "Heloise complex," a syndrome in which "a woman establishes herself as a philosopher's loving admirer; the situation is profitable to him and fatal to her" (162). Elsewhere, le Doeuff mocks these "whoeverians," and tells us: "I have long been doing my best to show that it is time for women to stop being the devoted followers of one (and always only one) coryphaeus" (59).

How does the image of the mother and of the bride operate, in *Hipparchia's Choice* and elsewhere in feminist discourse, to accomplish something that is unreachable by the argument alone? This is how, le Doeuff has warned us, we will know the philosophical imaginary:

> [T]he meaning conveyed by images works both for and against the system that deploys them. *For*, because they sustain something which the system cannot itself justify, but which is nevertheless needed for its proper working. *Against*, for the same reason, or almost: their meaning is incompatible with the system's possibilities. (1990, 3)

These two figures, of mother and bride, their intersection, and the involvement of le Doeuff's philosophical writing in the romance of feminism and philosophy, offer a chance to reflect on the place of sexual difference in philosophy and also in feminist theory. The erotics of seduction, of intellecual seduction, and more generally, of *the capture of theory by figure* seem to elude rational analysis. Le Doeuff's own concept of the philosophical imaginary can help us to pose these questions for feminist theory.

THE PRIMAL SCENE

What is the relation, then, between these two figures, of the mother and the bride? But in effect the figures are classically known, in culture and as a relation, as *two aspects of a wider scene.* This scene is one that le Doeuff herself characterizes, in her discussion of de Beauvoir's intellectual position, as a "primal scene."

The scene le Doeuff has in mind, between de Beauvoir and Sartre, is described by de Beauvoir in *Memoirs of a Dutiful Daughter,* and is interpreted according to the logic of the "primal scene" figure, as one of intellectual seduction, defloration, or even rape:

> One morning in the Luxembourg Gardens, near the Medici fountain, I outlined for him the pluralist morality which I

> had fashioned to justify the people I liked but did not wish to resemble: he ripped it to shreds. I was attached to it, because it allowed me to take my heart as the arbiter of good and evil; I struggled with him for three hours. In the end I had to admit I was beaten; besides, I had realized, in the course of our discussion, that many of my opinions were based only on prejudice, bad faith or thoughtlessness, that my reasoning was shaky and my ideas confused. "I'm no longer sure what I think, or even if I think at all," I noted, completely thrown . . . (1963, 380)

Le Doeuff questions her own desire in this part of her discussion of de Beauvoir, suggesting that she is perhaps placing herself in a textual position as de Beauvoir's younger sister. She even goes so far as to propose her own equivalent primal scene, at the secondary school in Brittany, where the philosophy teacher told her that *The Critique of Pure Reason* was too difficult for her, and set her instead a biography of Marie Curie. That may give us a nice explanation for the revenge she takes on Kant in the introduction to *The Philosophical Imaginary*, by finding his fear of castration at the origin of that intellectual enterprise.

But it is not as de Beauvoir's sister but as her daughter that le Doeuff would be figured in this primal scene, if it were one. Since le Doeuff has invoked the Freudian notion, let me first consider what, classically, the logic of the figure suggests. This primal scene, discovered by le Doeuff in the pages of a book, would cast de Beauvoir as the *mother* in the Luxembourg Gardens in a seduction witnessed (in the telling) by the child/reader. Laplanche and Pontalis summarize the psychoanalytic concept of the "primal scene" as: "Scene of sexual intercourse between the parents which the child observes, or infers on the basis of certain indication s, and phantasises. It is generally interpreted by the child as an act of violence on the part of the father" (1973, 335).

Since the primal scene is the child's scene, not the mother's, then this is *le Doeuff's* "primal scene," not de Beauvoir's, despite the way it is presented by le Doeuff in her text. And it is as the child that le Doeuff positions herself to witness a dreaded event already suspected in de Beauvoir's account of it, viz., the capture of this philosophical woman by this man.

The dreadful event is that *the father is the mother's lover*, which is to say that, despite the child's desire, the mother has a lover and it is the father. This is what a child "sees" in the primal scene. The truth is dreadful not because sex is a scandal for the child/reader—but because it undoes her own vain pre-Oedipal hopes for union with the mother.

The castration drama is frequently accompanied by a disavowal, in psychoanalyses of it; in *Hipparchia's Choice,* it brings on a textual invention in le Doeuff predictably aimed at denying the father/Sartre's power to do this. Le Doeuff employs the familiar "kettle logic" of the disavowal. Firstly, through the assertion of an "Heloise complex," the act is declared not to be a real act of love between de Beauvoir and Sartre. Secondly, through the arguments that discredit Sartre's own philosophy, the act is declared to be not a genuine one of love on "logical" grounds, that is, he couldn't be her desire, since he is not desirable. Her analysis of the failure of Sartre's philosophy to overpower her, in the manner the Luxembourg scene suggests he did, indeed presents him as impotent. Finally, through the suggestion that de Beauvoir herself had written a work of philosophy in *The Second Sex* that gave more to existentialism than it took from it, the act of love is denied in the third fashion of the "kettle defence," namely, it was not an act of love because, although it was strictly Sartre's penetration, such penetration was only possible because of *what de Beauvoir had given him.*

At this point, it can be said that de Beauvoir has been finally figured as the *phallic* mother. Psychoanalytic theory analyzes this image for the disavowal, as a figure whose impossibility can protect against the state of affairs depicted in the primal scene by affirming the moment before, when desire was intact. Le Doeuff devotes a significant amount of theoretical attention to *The Second Sex* as "mother's phallus," and its defense. She records that she corresponded with de Beauvoir about the reading of *The Second Sex* that she, le Doeuff desired to make, viz., that it is a work of philosophy that does not declare itself as such in order to protect male privilege in philosophy.

But, significantly, de Beauvoir refused to endorse this reading, or to denounce Sartre, and le Doeuff was left, she writes, to "sort it out for herself" (1991, 165). In refusing to confirm the interpretation that the feminist reader made of that scene, de Beauvoir possibly defended her own desire. Le Doeuff's analysis ignores the erotic in that heterosexual scene, despite the fact that there is a pleasure posited for de Beauvoir (and for Sartre) in his dominance and her submission. That it was de Beauvoir's *pleasure* is borne out by the fact that it is her story; she desired to write the scene in her memoir and, indeed, continuously wrote the mythology of their love.

Since de Beauvoir in effect refuses to interpret her own intellectual seduction as unequivocally an act of male violence, le Doeuff is propelled into intense intellectual curiosity (as Freud predicts), and the ensuing discussion in *Hipparchia's Choice,* of the place of sex in the subjectivity of philosophy, represents the outcome:

> To return once more to the Sartre/Simone "case," how did the emotional aspects and the modes of their relationship as lovers become fixed around an event. . . . *They were two students, a man and a woman, who were more or less equals in the university system, and yet, in being together, the first became the century's most visible philosopher and the second a tremendously well-hidden philosopher.* (138–139, my italics)

What will be the theoretical consequences, if they were two students, a man and a woman, *equal and yet* . . . ? In the primal scene, the reader encounters the problem of sexual difference.

A FEMINIST IMAGINARY

Despite le Doeuff's stated theoretical differences with psychoanalysis, she makes use of psychoanalytic concepts when she analyzes an Heloise "complex," when she evokes the notion of a "primal scene," and in the prospect of a philosophical "imaginary."

In *The Philosophical Imaginary*, she distinguishes the psychoanalytic from her own method: "The perspective I am adopting here differs, as will be seen, from both these approaches, since it involves reflecting on strands of the imaginary operating in places where, in principle, they are supposed not to belong and yet where, without them, nothing would have been accomplished" (1990, 2).

That heterogeneity can be contrasted with psychoanalytic approaches, including Freud's own, in which the primary process thinking of which reverie partakes, underlies rationality, and founds it. That there is a traffic between them may be what is most threatening to philosophy in the postulation of an unconscious.

The concept of a philosophical imaginary seems broadly psychoanalytic in at least the sense that it implies an intuition of "the unconscious": for it is the operation of an image deployed outside the author's conscious/ theoretical intent that is studied, along with its consequences, which, in terms of that consciousness that authors it, are ambivalent and unpredictable.

Le Doeuff also seems implicitly to accept a psychoanalytic account of the relation between desire and subjectivity, since her next question of an image in the text of philosophy is: What subjectivity is constructed by the figure as used? A desire is posited that can be satisfied in relation to an identity (although this isn't to claim she anywhere endorses a Lacanian picture of the subject).

There is one point, she writes, in an interpretation of an imaginary, where one "cannot do without a poetics, a psychoanalysis in the loose sense of the term." This is the point at which one answers the question: How does the image work, on the subjective level? (12). It follows that in seeking the explanation for the "affective charge" that an image carries, one needs to take up a theory of desire. Le Doeuff's reading of Kant's island, which begins her discussion of a specifically philosophical imaginary, is a psychoanalysis "in this loose sense," isolating the seduction and the "libidinal sacrifice" at work in the *Critique of Pure Reason.*

It is a certain affective charge on her own images that leads me to explore, "psychoanalytically," de Beauvoir as mother and bride in le Doeuff's book. An affective charge that almost amounts to rancor in other corners of *Hipparchia's Choice* provokes questions about the feminist theoretical enterprise which cannot be addressed through the notion of the reasonable alone. The reasonable is that which takes its force, by definition, in being justified; but the affective is a force (unlike the force of reason) which takes effect in an order unrelated to justification.

> [I]t seems doubtful to me whether any political or social force has ever had the power to make any circle of listeners whatsoever adopt a cultural product which did not answer a *question* meaningful to that social group. (20)

This question is clearly laid out, and covered over, by the image of the primal scene. As I have suggested, the scene brings to light the urgent question, "why a man and a woman, equal and yet . . . ?" Why would we be surprised to find that it is the question of sexual difference that animates the circle of feminist readers? The figures then, of mother, bride, and primal scene, operate (as le Doeuff argues of Kant's island) to picture a satisfaction for a reading subject, one that produces feminism as its consciousness.

In the philosophical imaginary, Le Doeuff finds herself torn between accusing the image in the philosophical text of standing for a tension in the theory, and of psychoanalyzing it as that which appears because its meaning is "incompatible with the system's possibilities." That which appears without warrant, as contradiction, to satisfy something the system cannot satisfy itself is itself a disavowal, in a quite technical sense; as something that serves to gratify a desire that is all the while denied.

Feminist consciousness, seeing the violence between men and women in characterizing the "struggle," does not necessarily seek to enforce a sexual repression that will keep the question of sex out of the feminist question of gender (despite what some critics believe). Rather, le Doeuff's analysis of de Beauvoir's book may deny the mother's desire, precisely because she has directed it so painfully away from the reader. The erotics of the primal scene might be said to *contradict* the reader's own desire, that desire for the mother figure expressed as jealousy for de Beauvoir.

The feminist attraction to the figure of de Beauvoir, through the image of the mother/bride, can be accounted for on these grounds as the disavowal of a desire. It is also the case that the satisfaction in representing her this way cannot be acccounted for "reasonably"—and this, too, the figure of the primal scene describes. At the very least, it cannot be done *reasonably* because of a lingering ambivalence in the sexual relation. The child, in viewing the primal scene, "perceives" a scene of apparent violence, when in fact, she witnesses the act of coitus; but do we reliably know the difference?

It is a difficult question, how to take up in feminist terms that ambivalence in heterosexuality that is related to the question of violence at the same time as it is related to the question of love. But it is a crucial one, since the opposition occurs at the center of feminist inquiry into its "subject," the nature of the sexual relation. In the primal scene the child makes a "mistake," a misinterpretation; and yet, one cannot completely leave the violent out of the act of love. We lack a feminist discussion of heterosexuality that approaches precisely this, the love *and* the violence found together.

Le Doeuff's reading puts aside the ambivalence of the sexual relation in order to protect the desire of the child/feminist. But the theoretical cost is that she can then only see the mother's desire for the father, in the heterosexual scene, as complicity in violence, and therefore the ambivalence returns as the query of "a man and a woman, equal and yet. . . ." This is a "return of the repressed" with real effects, some of which we are seeing in feminist politics currently: the resistance of some women to their "liberation," the disaffection of young women, the lack of satisfaction in the role of "career woman" and the exhausting remedy of the "superwoman."

This primal scene, presented as an *intellectual* seduction, is doubly problematic for feminism and for philosophy, since it raises the question how a woman could take pleasure in having her *mind* ravished. Not merely because this might imply that ideas are in our repertoire of sexual practices, and that a notion such as "sublimation" could be more carefully examined. But also the intellectual ravishment, as a sexual satisfaction depicted in his dominance and her submission, implies a sexualized mind, and a gendered rationality, two theoretical impossibilities in virtue of the very mind/body distinction through which they are produced.

Analysis of a feminist imaginary might lead us to explore the occurrence of transferences within feminist theory. Thinking feminism as a tradition draws us into the metaphors of "female relations," mother, sister, daughter. In pondering the relation, le Doeuff appropriates the philosophical desires of the mother-figure, or rather, in the case of de Beauvoir, overlooks that woman's antipathy to the role. De Beauvoir becomes surrounded by dutiful daughters, in the next theoretical generation, taking up this problem in the family all over again.

Perhaps it has been overlooked that relations to tradition (philosophical and otherwise, and however admirable) are relations to authority. When we invoke the mother-figure, do we know—and are we ready for—what will follow from it? As can be seen from this fragment of a "primal scene," anxiety about the maternal is reproduced in unpredictable ways at the level of theory.

Likewise, in courtship—in employing the metaphor, consciously and especially unconsciously—will we reproduce in theory the vexed power differentials between a man and a woman? Will we be able to conclude *anything other* than that we are abused? For, certainly, woman is not loved by philosophy.

And then again, "philosophy" is not a man, neither is "feminism" a woman. Even "woman" is not a woman, but a figure. Conceiving of the relation of women and philosophy on the model of a courtship forces the issue of sexual difference immediately. It may underline something important about the two, but it also occludes other possibilities. It blinds us to feminism as a historical moment, for example, or to philosophy as an art.

FIVE

Feminism Is a Kind of Time

If the feminism of slogans and figures lead to theoretical impasse, it is all the same possible to take the heretical sense of these possibilities, in theory and practice, and deduce at least *a kind of time* in which these could coincide.

Julia Kristeva, in her analysis of the tides of feminism in the essay *Women's Time,* has given a diagnosis of the "next moment" of feminism that is yet to be grappled with, even though that piece appeared first in French in 1979. Her vision takes in the panorama of three kinds of time, whose coincidence is both historical and conceptual. "There are three attitudes on the part of European feminist movements towards this conception of linear temporality, which is readily labelled masculine and which is at once both civilizational and obsessional" (1986, 193). Presented as historical actualities, Kristeva's description can nevertheless serve to describe moments in a conceptual scheme that has an appearance of necessity, or at least, that *has a logic to it.*

Kristeva's analysis begins from a first moment which she has also nominated as the first generation. "In its beginnings, the women's movement, as the struggle of suffragists and of existential feminists, aspired to gain a place in linear time as the time of project and history" (186, 193). This generation is probably the most familiar to Anglo-American feminists because it is where much of the discussion remains. These kinds of feminism, which in our own time encompass the aspirations of equal opportunity and "technological-rational" feminisms, are still very much extant and for good reason: they are projects, and continue to have goals, that are worth pursuing in relation to women's material-historical circumstances.

Nevertheless, as Kristeva notes, it has been a requirement of pursuing this kind of project that values belonging to "the time of project and history" have been adopted. In particular, it has been conceptually necessary for these feminisms to accept a version of the nation-state, and the narrative of the social contract, from which rights can be derived. Upholding the contract model, and thereby that particular moment of feminism, is the privilege given to consciousness and rationality.

That particular commitment leads this moment of feminism into its own impasse, and gives rise in Kristeva's analysis to a second time of feminism, a second generation, which nevertheless does not want to associate itself with, or identify itself in, the more linear or rational notion of time that she is proposing:

> In a second phase, linked, on the one hand, to the younger women who came to feminism after May 1968 and, on the other, to women who had an aesthetic or psychoanalytic experience, linear temporality has been almost totally refused, and as a consequence there has arisen an exacerbated distrust of the entire political dimension (194).

This second generation of feminism has dwelt more in the realm of the unconscious, and sometimes, through its leftist leanings, has understood it as false consciousness. In analyses of womens' position, it has sought theoretical inspiration in terms of (post)structuralist, psychoanalytic, or other "hermeneutics of suspicion." "Essentially interested in the specificity of female psychology and its symbolic realization, these women seek to give a language to the intra-subjective and corporeal experiences left mute by culture in the past," and, "by demanding recognition of an irreducible identity, without equal in the opposite sex and, as such, exploded, plural, fluid, in a certain way non-identical, this feminism situates itself outside the linear time of identities . . . " (194).

It is not surprising to discover that these two moments in feminism, where they occur together, find themselves in conflict. This might even be predicted from the simple evidence that the conscious-unconscious division is conceived as a conflictual structure, by definition. Kristeva follows the trajectories of these generations, in terms of what is perhaps most alarming about each of them.

For the feminism of consciousness, a kind of dissipation has resulted from the impotence of rationality and the general "enlightenment project." This Kristeva describes as "a certain exhaustion of its potential as a programme for a new social contract" (197), an exhaustion occuring in historical terms as a loss of impetus for further moves to economic, political, and professional equality—the famed "backlash." It can be seen in terms of a conceptual limitation, viz.: That since this feminism shares with its Enlightenment context (socialist and democratic government) a commitment to equality, "the specific character of women could only appear as non-essential or even non-existent to the totalising and even totalitarian spirit of this ideology" (ibid.).

For the second moment, the feminism of the unconscious encounters the constant magnetism of violence (rhetorical and otherwise), in which the unconscious finds expression in a technological-rational world. Kristeva's analysis scans the attraction of certain kinds of separatism, and (worse materially, and for the practice of feminism) to certain kinds of terrorism (she discusses them from examples such as the Bader-Meinhoff, which were relevant in France at the time of writing but which in no way render her insight redundant in the present).

But Kristeva's explanation of a "symbolic contract" explains why the second moment, in retreating from equality to specificity, may identify vehemently with the sacrificial aspect of sexual difference, and break itself (and others) in its frustration. For Kristeva, the metaphorology of castration, which belongs to the imaginary of psychoanalysis, nevertheless designates a logical hypothesis from which the character of our general psychosocial predicament can be deduced.

Her symbolic contract is defined in contrast to the social contract of the first generation: "[T]he social contract, far from being that of equal men, is based on an essentially sacrifical relationship of separation and articulation of differences which in this way produces communicable meaning" (199). Language, a "separation from a presumed state of nature," introduces an "articulated network of differences," a network of substitutes for the objects for which its signs stand and through which meaning comes about (198). This view she presents as "Freudian" but is more attributable in the Anglophone context to Lacan, and the figure of sacrifice is shared with other structuralist accounts of culture and subjectivity.

To the extent that feminism as a political philosophy inherits the problems of liberalism and of the Enlightenment, it will encounter an intensification of violence *alongside* the intensification of rationality, and even consequent upon it. Kristeva implies at the end of her paper that one cannot guard against either of those possibilities—neither a hyperrationality nor the irrational as expressed violently—and in either of these moments, *while one remains unconscious of them.* Nevertheless, the demands of dismantling conceptual commitments involve transformation, maybe even of cherished political norms, and this naturally causes anxiety.

But anxiety is recognizable as the other side of desire—in this case, a desire for a certain metaphysical view of the nature of things to be upheld. It might mean that a repressed element of the theory cannot remain so—there will be the "bringing to light," to use the psychoanalytic metaphor, of the unconscious of feminist theory, which would be an awkward and difficult task, and one which the normativity of feminist practice would resist. But this resistance demonstrates a feature of normative theories in general, that they desire that their truth be accepted literally, rather than scrutinized at a second order.

Where does Kristeva's diagnosis of our time leave us? Or, as she puts it another way: *"What can be our place in the symbolic contract?"* She proposes a third generation, one that we are yet to inhabit effectively, and one that is not quite present, nor even quite a future perhaps; certainly utopian. Feminisms, where they have already broached this moment, have taken other philosophies with them, and have led the way. This third moment Kristeva writes of as the "demassification of difference," and she describes it simply as coming to recognize the masculine-feminine distinction—and all other kinds of distinction—as *belonging to metaphysics.*

SUBJECTIVITY AND SEXUATE "GENRE"

A different understanding of sexual difference emerges in the work of rhetorician Luce Irigaray, which provides an opportunity for the thought of gender as genre.

There is an established discussion in feminist theory of subjectivity and its inherent sexedness. Already, the apparently self-evident propositions of a style of rational thought screen a division and a subordination that have been exhaustively described. To take up only one example, psychoanalytic feminism has detailed the logic of sexual distinction as a founding distinction for rationality. The analysis of the logic of the copula can be pursued through a concept of "genre" that explicitly links sexual difference to a politics of representation. I take up this question in chapter 9 (and cf. Ferrell 2000).

In *Thinking the Difference*, Luce Irigaray discusses the import of grammar to the forms of thinking about logical and sexual identity.

> The *fort/da* that Freud describes as the child's entry into the world of language and culture does not work properly for the girl, except through identification with the boy. The little

> girl becomes alienated in someone other than herself and makes quasi-objects of her children. . . . Confusing identity and identification is not the same thing as finding an order for the matter and form that we are. Confusing them is an idealistic delusion that produces a great deal of social entropy. That is where the neuter is often located: in the confusion between identity and identification. (19)

"Irigaray, by adopting the term genre, wants to give a new sense to belonging to 'men' and 'women' as sexuate identities," writes Penelope Deutscher in *A Politics of Impossible Difference* (2002). "This intention is lost where the term is rendered by the English 'gender' " (and cf. de Lauretis, *Technologies of Gender,* 1987, 4–5). Deutscher refers to this aspect of "genre" in a reading of Irigaray that captures the sense of law or representation in it. As she puts it, "Irigaray considers that women as a symbol and as a group have been exploited in the representation of masculinity" (2002, 75, my italics). Identity is a representational order—in this Irigaray depicts the Lacanian view—in which the subject recognizes *himself.* To say "herself" would be to bring forward the analysis at once, because it is the exclusion of the feminine from representation as subject which is at issue:

> Speaking of sexuate genre in *Thinking the Difference* (1994), Irigaray comments that "woman must be able to express herself in words, images and symbols in this intersubjective relationship with her mother, then with other women, if she is to enter into a non-destructive relationship with men." (20)

The impossibility at work in genre is seen in the way it bisects sexual difference by two kinds, male and female, while at the same time, by that very work, revealing the representational field of gender to be possibly multiple. The reading of sexual difference as multiple, finding its inspiration in poststructuralist philosophy, is also presently made by feminists such as Judith Butler, and Irigaray's adherence to *two* genres has led some to suggest her work has a "heterosexist" bias.

Deutscher, addressing this, asks what would secure the boundaries of the genres as "two"; that is, why for Irigaray, the necessity of two asserts itself, when for others multiplicity answers a theoretical need. Referring to Kelly Oliver's analysis on this point, Deutscher answers for Irigaray that the figure of "two" corrects the logic of the self-same "one," the "sex-neutral" humanity of Western thought. Oliver, too, argues that "two" genres are not equivalent, and their differences cannot be sublated in a Hegelian dialectic.

This logic of sexual difference may be what provokes Irigaray to write, in *The Ethics of Sexual Difference*, that sexual difference is the question of the age (1993, 1). Her deconstructive sensibility means that, as Deutscher argues, while she situates "relation to multiplicity at the heart of each genre," she resists conceiving of multiple genres. "This reluctance has important implications for her understanding of cultural difference" (2002, 187), Deutscher concludes. But, through her insistence on this ambivalence in the form of impossible difference, social reform in Irigarayan thought can be figured in terms of the *reimagination and reinvention* of difference. In coming to represent the question of sexual difference as political, Deutscher argues that Irigaray's work advocates that we uphold a value of difference and that public policy not be confined to a "politics of recognition." This is not, however, the vacuous affirming of "any and every kind of difference." Her thinking through the impossible difference of the other "suggests that we should attend most to those differences that hegemonic cultural forces are most invested in excluding" (186).

Deutscher continues a theme she began in her earlier *Yielding Gender*, the exploration of "operative contradiction." In relation to Irigaray's later work, this takes shape in her analysis as the working out of "impossible difference." Deutscher wants to associate the philosophical with the political, to tie Irigaray's concepts to her politics, an enterprise that Irigaray has long stood for in the Anglo-canon, through her incarnation as a "French feminist philosopher."

It is not clear that Irigaray herself has always subscribed to the distinction between a philosophy and a politics. Between them stands her practice, psychoanalysis, which has its own therapeutic aims. They are not always in accord either with the consciousness of philosophy, nor the agency of feminism/politics. If there is a tolerance for the impossible in Irigaray's philosophy-politics, it arises from this third term, the ambiguity and ambivalence in the unconscious understood (following Lacan) as a playing out of drives in signification.

But does Irigaray follow Lacan, whose pupil she was at one stage? That influence, too, is ambivalent. The answer seems to be: she does, and she doesn't. Writes Deutscher: "Luce Irigaray generates a feminist politics through the affirmation of a concept of sexual difference as both possible and impossible, without and (in the form of its own exclusion) within culture" (185). This is a Lacanian view, on one level; the utilizing of the feminine as a mute persistence in the Other, outside signification. Yet, in Irigaray's hands, it famously transforms itself from a conservative narcissistic mysogyny into a politics of sexual difference:

> Irigaray recently suggested that her work could be divided into three phases. There was, she explains, a first, critical phase, of decentering the dominance of a masculine perspective on the world. There was a second phase, of defining "those mediations that could permit the existence of a feminine subjectivity." A new, third phase corresponds to the construction of an intersubjectivity respecting sexual difference. Here, the governing question would be "how to define a philosophy . . . an ethic, a relationship between two different subjects?" (97)

Deutscher's reading of Irigaray is ever respectful, generous in what it gives to the text in allowing for both its strengths and its instabilities. This is perhaps the only way to read a philosophical writer such as Irigaray, who is so attuned to the imaginary and so effective in her engagement of genre, both literary and sexuate.

For example, Irigaray often deploys the utopian, a rhetorical device mistaken for a propositional intent by readers who charge her with "essentialism." But as Deutscher reads her:

> Irigaray offers an ideal image of a mediated, peaceful, loving, differentiated, and nonhierarchical relationship between self and other. Certainly, we can interpret this ideal in many ways. For example, it can be seen as emphasizing the impossibility of such a relationship. Perhaps it acts to provoke us to reflect on the reasons for this impossibility. We may also wish to ask whether it is the right ideal. Perhaps an emphasis on the inevitablity of aggression, appropriation, and narcissism and the need for us to avow and negotiate these forces would be more appropriate? Certainly, insofar as Irigaray understands sexual difference, friendship and love to be appropriative, she also imagines that our figurings of women, friends and lovers bear the trace of exclusion of their broader possibilities, which are simultaneously acknowledged and disavowed by us. (186)

For Irigaray, like Kristeva, an understanding of sexual difference leads to the critique of metaphysics that is a feature of contemporary philosophy. "In order to make it possible to think through, and live, this difference, we must reconsider the whole problematic of *space* and *time*" (7).

It leads her to proclaim in *The Ethics of Sexual Difference*: "Sexual difference is one of the major philosophical issues, if not the issue, of our age" (1993, 5). In philosophical terms (and she flags this when she mentions Heidegger in the next sentence) this can be argued by pointing up how humanist assumptions are confounded by an organic difference *within* the human. Even if humanism is merely a disguise for Western chauvinism, it is still confounded by this presence of difference within it that it is made up of two kinds, men and women.

Irigaray cites more utopian uses for her claim: "Think of it [sexual difference] as an approach that would allow us to check the many forms that destruction takes in our world"; "Sexual difference would constitute the horizon of worlds more fecund than any known to date—at least in the West—and without reducing fecundity to the reproduction of bodies and flesh" (1993, 5).

In these polemics, Irigaray draws both on Heidegger's critique of technology and on possibilities suggested by Lacan's "imaginary anatomy," and she brings logic and the erotic together as two parts of one project. This is a captivating synthesis of philosophy, psychoanalysis, and feminism—not to mention of the poetics of philosophy and polemic. Indeed, she promises that sexual difference can also create "a new poetics" for a new age.

> The transition to a new age requires a change in our perception and conception of *space-time*, the *inhabiting of places*, and of *containers*, or *envelopes of identity* . . .

This is because the history of space-time has been the history of the subject, as Irigaray sketches. Time with Kant becomes finally "the interiority of the subject itself," and thereby consciousness; while space becomes its exteriority. In order to get at this "difference" that is heralded in sexual difference, without reducing it automatically to *something* and therefore to something exterior and other, Irigaray sees that it will be necessary to take apart the structures that give "things" in their "reality" their identity.

In present sexual relations, Irigaray tells us, "what is missing is the double pole of attraction and support, which excludes disintegration or rejection, attraction and decomposition, but which instead ensures the separation that articulates encounter and makes possible speech, promises, alliances." Here she makes use of psychoanalytic practice, of the "psychical container" that the maternal relation, or the analytic situation, is said to offer to the growing healing subjectivity. The positive model of "attraction and support" that can ensure mutual recognition between subjects is contrasted with the subject that, acting alone, finds another subject to be merely exterior, and expels her. It diagnoses the theoretical problem for the sexual relation. The "double pole" of attraction and support describes ambivalence in a positive sense, as an operation that both allows for identification and for distinction. But this is not the notion of ambivalence as conceived by, for example, Freud, who took a colder view.

Can this analysis be extended to the problem of relation as such, as it occurs in the logic of identity, that is, are all oppositional relations in need of this moment of recognition? Because the maternal bond is an originating event in the personal history of subjectivity, contemporary psychoanalysis, and feminist psychoanalysis in particular, tends to make of the maternal the *history of the origin* of the subject. Thereby, it makes the assumption that the dichotomy of masculine and feminine is an original or founding opposition. Both Irigaray and Kristeva assume a version of this.

But while sexual difference (in the Oedipus complex) may emerge as archaic in the individual, as that which in fact triggers the process of symbolization, it does not thereby give it *conceptual priority*, let alone make it a causal origin of dichotomous thought. In theory, the distinctions that carry such psychical influence—self/world; subject/object; masculine/feminine—are analogous, probably mutually reinforcing, but only causal as a matter of history, not of time as such.

To imagine that historical time can make conceptual relations causal in this way (for example, difference from the mother leads to difference from the world) is to confuse the *genres* of historical and theoretical time. Concepts do not need history; we cannot find conceptual priority in original distinctions. *Distinction itself* is the problematic of the copula, the figure of logical distinction, and sexual difference along with logical difference find their expression in this pro forma of identity.

Another way of saying this is to point out that our thinking is more than our history of thinking, since "the past is never past," as Irigaray quotes. Indeed, the past is an imaginary space of critical importance in the thought of the present. And, more than this, the originating distinction for the purely conceptual structure of identity could not be found, and it need not be. We may learn it "causally" in a personal temporal sequence or history; however, our web of meanings need not be imagined as having a beginning or ending, but may rather be thought of as seamless and circular.

The new age of sexual difference "assumes and entails an evolution or a transformation of forms, of the relations of *matter* and *form* and of the interval *between* . . . " (7), Irigaray writes. Understanding the economy of the interval requires a concept of time that will scrutinize itself as the *effect of interval.* But how, in this sense, can we have a "new age" at all? Where, in the economy of the interval, can we find the new, the novel, the utopian, and the original?

In Irigaray's own polemic, this issue is not resolved, since she writes that sexual difference, as the bearer of difference as such, would provoke a revolution of something *new*, the defeat of the logic of identity. This is something without a historical precursor. How can, on the one hand, a historical continuity of sexual relations, and on the other, the logic of necessity, be reconciled? Irigaray's new poetics will carry this paradoxical double burden. I look again at this question through the concept of "genre" in chapter 9.

In her utopian vision of a moment in which difference is experienced as attraction and offered as support, can Irigaray reconcile her psychoanalytic with her deconstructive insight? It is a question of a poetics—whether that part of her philosophy which brings us to a critical understanding of the production of value, including of sexual difference, undermines her rhetorical sea-change, toward romance, metaphor, and passions such as wonder.

The new of Irigaray's "new age" may be a utopian solution of paradox. And what might look like an attempt in Kristeva at synthesis—the generations of feminism expressed in the classic logic of threes, which governs the dialectic—may prove on closer inspection to be a chimera. If I use metaphors of improbablity—utopia, chimera—in discussing Kristeva's third moment and Irigaray's new age, it is because it seems important that these timely notions be genuinely improbable, at least in logical terms. And it is important that they be improbable, not as spectral impossibilities, but as living occurrences of breached legibility. (Deutscher analyzes this effect in the case of Irigaray as '"a politics of impossible difference" and in de Beauvoir, as "operative contradiction.") The utopic is a *genre*, and not a time or place, despite its presentation as one.

How can a position simultaneously demand and refuse a notion of history, or of reason? But it is precisely this unthinkable position that is given to women in the paradox of the symbolic order, as both Kristeva and Irigaray in various places argue. She must find herself *only as exterior* to the subject: "She" is a paradox. The conception of time and/or reason is both impossible and unavoidable, as are all metaphysical oppositions, and this is precisely why the question of genre, that is, of representation as ineluctably oppositional, need be raised. We need not waste time seeking the coherence of this attitude within a usual rational scheme, but rather, try to find other philosophical resources to depict the occurrence of paradox differently. In their difference styles, Kristeva's "symbolic contract" and Irigaray's "new poetics" both approach the mirage of opposition.

The investigation of this metaphysics calls for sexual difference to be analyzed as itself a logic. Beyond the Oedipus story, the castration figure that Kristeva herself uses and which has preoccupied theoretical attention for the question of this "symbolic contract," there are other figures that are less tractable but have potential in the process of theorizing difference. The rhetorical procedure known to psychoanalysis as the *disavowal* particularly suggests itself, because of its special relation to the logic of opposition. In analyzing masculine and feminine as part of that logic, it is necessary to recruit a conceptual understanding that can include that which is "repressed" by the distinction, to wit, that which it has excluded in order to install itself. This cannot be done within familiar philosophical logic, since it is itself part of the operation of distinction. But the logic of the disavowal would have as its whole purpose the representation of the ambivalent moment, one in which "it is and it isn't." Ambivalence is exactly what opposition aims to "fix," in fixing a value (but cf. Butler 1998). If logic, as Heidegger promises us, is to be about the *thinkable possibility,* we may reflect that the repressed is precisely the *unthinkable*; that which must be obscured, in order for the definition to go ahead.

It has been said of the case of "repressed memory," for example, that the incest victim is not living with the "unknown thought" so much as with the "unthought known" (cf. Rose 2004). As a configuration of the repressed, it is a challenge to render this as logic. Likewise, to render that "double movement" of the third moment, or generation, of feminism, or the new age of sexual difference, remains a rhetorical hope rather than a conceptual event.

To connect time with feminism will also connect it to a history of ideas. This is something empirical feminism resists; and yet, it needs to be done in order to take up the notion of sexual difference as a metaphysical one. For sexual difference to have been revealed as a metaphysical question is a significant moment for feminism and for philosophy. It is a moment when an empirical history of suffering discerns its theoretical gravity, and the particular contingent protest becomes a general conceptual challenge. From this moment, an account might begin of the startling conceptual vigor of feminist philosophy, which has had an influence well beyond the domesticated sphere to which the (male-dominated) philosophical institution desires to confine it.

But the failure to appreciate time as paradox leads to the intellectual truncation of feminism. The seduction of the objective and external look of time leads to taking its progress literally. This is to misunderstand the problem of sexual difference completely. The revolutionary story of liberation from an oppressive past into a better future (precious though it is) can blind feminism into thinking itself as *more than history*, as a messianic moment in which women's state is changed forever. Whereas the deepest and most wounding problem in sexual difference is the one expressed in the cry: "*Why*, in all times and all places . . . ?" Sexual oppression has been reinvented at every moment, and this is what makes sexual difference the metaphysical question of our age. But if feminism is thought without thinking through this paradox of time, the idea of liberation seems less and less plausible.

What would remain of a feminist moment that has conceded that its object of enquiry—the feminine, and the sexual relation—is a kind of logical fiction? Can the paradox of the third generation and the new age happen anyway, despite being implausible? Other modern revolutions show that liberation is both an enduring hope and a fleeting moment in history. Such is the irony of event, that sometimes what is released is no longer recognizable. What will the feminist moment, in time, have liberated?

Some contemporary feminist discussions of this problematic go via the work of phenomenologists such as Levinas and Heidegger. Rosalyn Diprose, for example, in *Corporeal Generosities* employs a sustained reading of this tradition in her analysis of the political scene. Tina Chanter, too, in her book *Time, Death and the Feminine,* addresses the question of how to relate feminism to metaphysics and how to do a philosophical feminism. She does so, both through a critique of the rhetoric of philosophy in Levinas's notions of the "saying" and the "said," and through a critique of the possibility of translating metaphysical concerns into political applications.

"I am struggling to negotiate a delicate path between textual exegesis and schematic research," she writes (2002, xi), a negotiation that comes with a risk. This risk Chanter is "willing to take," in order to challenge the timidity of exegesis that will not confront social and political concerns, as well as the arrogance of "issue-oriented research," which would dismiss philosophers such as Heidegger and Levinas as "having anything intelligible or meaningful to say about the world" (xii).

The distinction Chanter is making is between an implied defense of reading and textuality as a method of political engagement and the strangely gendered space of metaphysics, that often seems to relish its lack of application to real world purposes. The opposition between exegesis and the addressing of issues, between metaphysics and politics, is inflamed in the case of Levinas's critique of Heidegger, the one being a Jewish scholar, the other a National Socialist sympathizer. Quoting

Lacoue-Labarthe and Nancy, Chanter notes that to speak of a "logic of fascism" is to say that "a certain logic is fascist, and that this logic is not wholly foreign to the general logic of rationality inherent in the metaphysics of the subject" (7).

The problem arises with a style of rationality that begins in Western metaphysics as the opposing of the subject to its object, and ends with the generalizing of the subject's purposes to the means/ends thinking of instrumental rationality. This rationality or logic is famously critiqued by Heidegger where this temporality is also challenged (and cf. chapter 9).

> The idea that things in the world and human beings are fundamentally ontologically similar—that they have basically the same kind of being—has been taken to suggest that the same kind of knowledge is appropriate for both types of things. Hence, there is an epistemological bias toward a scientific model, whereby science is deemed to be an adequate type of knowledge for the study of human beings, just as it is considered a legitimate method of inquiry for questions concerning the reality of natural objects.

The logic that finds itself in this "copula" form, positing subject and object, generalizes its own time to suit the schema of this distinction. But the time that underpins the logic of this subject is paradoxical:

> [O]n the one hand, there is an assumption that the now, or present moment, is the most real. On the other hand, there is the opposing assumption that permanence, endurance, or that which lasts (as opposed to that which is in flux or transition, that which passes away in becoming, rather than being), has the most reality. Since the now, by its very nature, passes or is transitory, these two assumptions cannot both hold—unless there is an unacknowledged recourse to an idea of eternity, understood as an eternal now. (16)

This "privileging of the present" engenders a circularity, says Heidegger, in which philosophers since the time of the Greeks

> take time itself as one entity among others, and try to grasp it in the structure of its Being, though that way of understanding Being which they have taken as their horizon is one which is itself naively and inexplicitly oriented toward time.

Chanter notes the implication of time in this constitution of the subject and its object shows itself in the politics of the day: "One of the problems that feminist and race theorists confront is the need to take account of the historical nature of their own discourses" (16).

> Rather than lamenting the fact that Heidegger's thought is insufficiently rigorous, and suggesting that it is this failure to live up to the high standards of traditional philosophy that underlies his Nazi involvement, Levinas reverses the logic of implication . . . he asks whether it is the very standards held dear by the tradition of philosophy itself that are at fault. (7)

Going farther, Levinas criticizes Heidegger for staying within a tradition that gives priority to *being* in the analysis of time:

> a tradition that, whether it sees time as objective or subjective, always conceives of time in a solitary subject. Traditional philosophy. . . remained with the conception of a time either taken to be purely exterior to the subject, a time-object, or taken to be entirely contained in the subject. But the subject in question was always a solitary subject. (28)

Thus, in his thinking of being and of time, Chanter argues, Heidegger is charged by Levinas with prioritizing ontology over ethics, which is to say, giving priority to the logic of the same over the logic of the other.

Chanter links these metaphysical concerns with time and ontology to the "obstinacy" of a certain concept of history through Levinas's concern for language, and the action of philosophy. In his relating of the "saying" to the "said," Chanter sees him setting up a rhetorical necessity for philosophy to recast its problems at every instant, allowing the action of the "saying" to disturb the surface of the "said":

> I will suggest that there is a necessary betrayal involved in the very attempt to do philosophy, and that this betrayal concerns the very function of language as thematization. It is the task of language to betray what it also expresses—and in the function of language as expression there lies hope. Since language is never fixed, since it constantly eludes synchrony, such hope cannot be fixed; it can only be renewed in the diachrony of discourse. The rhythmic alternative of language between the "saying" and the "said" incessantly unsettles the sedimentation of the "said." (226)

The diachrony of reflection is built into philosophy, and explains why it must continue its "saying"—on politics, on ethics, on social sciences, etc.—and not give way to the discourses of the logic of scientific time and the subject. It is through this diachrony, Chanter argues, that we can understand why Levinas is not "violating the essence of the egalitarian or democratic ideal," even as he "construes ethical responsibility as asymmetrical and unequal."

However, turning to the feminine as a measure of this alterity, Chanter finds the diachrony may or may not forestall a foreclosure on the other. Chanter argues that Levinas uses the figures of the feminine to achieve a depiction of an alternate concept/experience of time, the "lapse of time irrecuperable in the temporalization of time" which will become not merely the pathos of something lost, but a source of something new (244). But:

> What accounts for Levinas's insistence on the inequality of my relation to others, the incommensurability of this relation, and how can this inequality be thought "in a sense absolutely opposed to oppression"? (225)

The feminine in *Totality and Infinity*, and maternity in *Otherwise than Being* presides over that which will be borne out in responsibility for the other, she argues (244):

> In the strategic role that is performed by maternity, which allows the textual progression to justice, to the third party, to the birth of thought (see TI 128; Tel 101), but which itself does not measure up to the demands of justice, we have begun to see that the formal problem that Levinas confronts in sustaining the claims that he want to make about time is also reflected in his use of the language of sexual difference. (245)

A "saying" confronts a "said," which is how Chanter conceives of the deployment of this language of sexual difference, and which saves it from the blunt appropriation of the figures of woman for a project that keeps us in our metaphysical place. Nevertheless, since we do not have complete mastery in the "saying," it isn't guaranteed that such oppression would not still eventuate—and perhaps in the instance of the feminine, Levinas is not sufficiently attentive to the passage of his "saying" into the "said."

> Maternity both describes "responsibility for others" (OB 106; AE 135), as a "complete being 'for the other'" (OB 108; AE

> 137), and at the same time it remains on the hither side of thought and consciousness, always preparatory. It can "slip toward" knowledge, but it is not yet knowledge. (245)

Furthermore, since "sexual specificity" is no mere rhetorical flourish but is a "structuring theme of Levinas's discourse" (250), then we can call Levinas to account for what he does for, and with, the feminine mode of existence:

> Levinas's understanding of the feminine as a disruption of the virile categories of mastery, domination, and self-possession opens up the possibility of another way of (non)being. . . . The feminine functions as a critique of Heidegger, and it is under the sign of the feminine that Levinas explores sensibility, materiality, and the corporeal, which remain undeveloped in Heidegger's analysis. (251)

Indeed, Chanter emphasizes that it is Levinas's argument, through these figures, that Heidegger neglects the otherwise than being *in his neglect* of the feminine, the maternal and the sensible.

So, while these aspects of his text open a space for the rethinking of the feminine, other aspects appear to close it down. Even the metaphorical use of the feminine "does not mean that the resonance of these sexualized terms is not felt in the world," and however Levinas might accept the risk of any "saying," "as a notion that signifies beyond and despite his 'said,'" he cannot by his own argument exempt himself from responsibility for what is said through his saying (252).

Chanter's argument in effect charges Levinas with a *rhetorical* oppression that is particularly suggestive. "The problem of the feminine comes into play at three different levels," she writes: "First there is the textual movement facilitated or set in motion by the feminine, and brought to a resolution, completion, or closure by paternity" (254). Only at this level is the masculine figure the clear beneficiary of the textual work of the feminine. But: "Second, there is the formal or structural function of the feminine as it is invoked as an exception to being, as a breakdown of the systematicity of thought, as an interruption of totality." The subject, implicitly masculine, but generalized to all, is disturbed by the feminine in a way very familiar to readers of other texts of Western philosophy.

> Finally, there is the paradigmatic role that the feminine plays as preliminary, as a first sketch of the ethical, as a kind of

> prolegomenon. . . . Yet this preparatory role cannot be acknowledged as such, since to do so would be to lessen the radicality of the ethics it announces.

In this, Chanter finds the feminine to be integral in the metaphysics as representation of that difficulty Levinas confronts in claiming "that the present can signify outside representation, or that diachrony is irreducible to the synchronization of thematization, or that the 'saying' goes beyond the 'said,' is otherwise than essence" (255).

And, in this portrait of the dilemma, Chanter clarifies a feminist discomfort with Levinas as one in which to have the "indetermination, ambiguity, equivocation, diachrony," "the delightful lapse in being," one also must accept that one is "allowing the feminine to do its work in the absence of recognition," an all-too-ordinary posture with little that is radical about it.

I think it matters to point out that the consequence of this textual style of critique of Levinas, is that his *logic* is revealed as flawed. His "otherwise than being" may fail to persuade the solitary subject he was setting out to counter, since the radical alterity is not accomplished, but is only produced through a repression. But can one excise the feminine figures from the model of alterity? It is implicit in Chanter's argument that one cannot, since they structure the diachrony that the "saying" and the "said" provokes.

Returning to the question of exegesis and its value to a politics: what does it do for "history" to reflect on "time"? What does the reading of Levinas's metaphysical argument with Heidegger say to feminism? Chanter suggests that making the "painstaking" reading of Heidegger and Levinas will advance the politics, by examining a conceptual framework and offering its scaffolding to some contemporary impasses; specifically, in the case of Levinas, that his critique of time as diachrony is simultaneously a critique of the representation of being and specifically the (non)being of woman.

Is the resulting structure revealed as supportive of a kind of feminist demand, or will the load-bearing function of the feminine go unacknowledged? Is Levinas "half-right" about the feminine—or is his work "worse than nothing," for returning women to their original place in things, in the service of a father-son conglomerate, which appears as a narcissistic subject?

Or, rather, does such an exegesis perform the function of questioning a kind of *feminist* theoretical demand? One of the unacknowledged aspects of the rationalist versus postmodernist "tangle" that earlier Chanter identifies is the foreshortening of a conceptual critique of politics in the name of its ethical urgency. While Levinas displays an ethics that precedes ontology, a very important insight for the challenging of the self-evidence of the subject and its copulative objectifying, he does not thereby place *philosophy* after ethics.

The critique of the "saying" and the "said" places the diachrony of reflection at the ethical moment, just as much as it does at the ontological one (in which the subject constitutes itself against a background). This idea of time—an ethics *before* an ontology—is already a "said" that calls on, and for, a "saying." In other words, wherever philosophy is a "saying," there it calls into question time, and history.

This point is critical for feminism, because it interrogates the production of *feminist* values—as history, and as its several charges against justice—just as much as it calls to account the "egology" of the prevailing subject-in-time, whose scientism cannot face the other as otherwise than as an object for present purposes. So working with Levinas's texts as material for feminist reflection has been doubly instructive in Chanter's text; his "saying" teaches feminist thinking about diachrony, while his "said" provides the provocation necessary for the feminist "saying" in reply.

The anxiety about the exegetical has also conventionally been about the viability of "being faithful" to a text, conjuring a submissive posture in relation to a master-discourse. This method has offended some feminists because it has seemed to reflect the contour of heterosexual submission too closely (cf. Michele le Doeuff's "whoeverians"). And Chanter asks, How can she be faithful to the text of an author who has declared that there is no substitute for oneself?

Perhaps the "hours of painstaking reading" supply the corrective to this impression; in the "enjoyment of reading and the curiosity of studying in order to come to know the world" which Chanter finds explicit in Levinas's portrait of sensibility. The sheer pleasure of exegesis is strictly unrecuperable in the time of reason and project, even of the feminist project. The reader does not tread the "delicate path" only to arrive somewhere politically accomplished; she reads in an evanescent present which will be lost to future purposes, as it will be to history. The pleasure of reading exceeds the time of politics, just as if that delicate path meandered. As if, even should it turn out that it all meant nothing and went nowhere, it would still otherwise satisfy.

The problematic of the "saying" and the "said" is a fruitful moment for an interruption of philosophy into feminism; of feminist-inspired philosophy into philosophy. In adjuring ethics to take up philosophy, Chanter's argument reflects on Levinas's desire to prevent the "said" from becoming the truth and the law, even while it is inevitable and necessary that it will do so. This is the irresolvable ambivalence, indicating an ambiguity, that the question of time as diachrony allows.

Feminist philosophy as just such a "call to book," is paradoxically a call to politics not to fix on the "said," and a call to philosophy to interrupt the sediment of its thought in the cause of justice (here, the justice demanded by gender). The readings Chanter lays out show a feminist philosophy in which politics is not enough, since it demands we interrupt the "said," and interrupt in the hope that time will thereby interrupt history, forcing on it new terms including new terms of expression.

SIX

The Lore of the Father

"Feminism of equality" has been so successful that it has resulted in unparalleled opportunities for participation by women in the public sphere, and even in philosophy. This democracy must be considered gratifying, but its effects have been multiple and unpredictable, tending to fall outside what can be captured in the "equal opportunity" philosophy that in part engendered it.

Perhaps the briefest summary of those effects could be this: women have found, in occupying the same places as men in a man's world, that nevertheless they occupy them differently. Equal opportunity promotes the theoretical equivalence of the terms *man* and *woman* so that they can do the same work and receive the same benefits, but precisely because of this, it does not understand sexual difference as other than denigration. This startling effect is still being denied by proponents of that feminism or, rather, is being denied its theoretical significance.

Some feminists have turned their attention to the question of sexual difference, recognizing that sexual difference is a bodily difference and that it is the body that has been overlooked in the traditional analyses of equality. The patriarchal practices that make up the lived reality of being men or women operate according to the difference between bodies, assigning them a place. This, it has been concluded, explains why, even when in his place, the woman of equal opportunity finds that she differs.

But proposing the question of sexual difference in relation to the body has brought feminist theory up against the operations of theory;

for example, its oppositional effect in the assumption of a distinction between "things in the real world" and "the interpretations" theory gives of them. The body, on this distinction, is classed with things, and held to be inured in its substance from the interpretations made of it. The body has been held to be a mute physical given, lying outside, but suffering under, social discourses.

Analyses of sexual difference as being somehow "of the body" are from this perspective easy to accuse of essentialism and/or determinism. But the separation of the body from theory has happened as a consequence of the distinction, leading to the curious paradox that the very thing that sexual difference cannot afford to be about, in feminist theory, is the difference between men's and women's bodies.

At this point, what may become visible is not the picture, but the frame: the investigation moves from asking questions about the "signified" of feminist theory (i.e., women's subordination) to asking questions about the theoretical "signifier" itself. And this very distinction, between signified and signifier, proposes its own commitments: asking questions of discourse as discourse takes feminist theory through the looking glass of deconstruction.

In her critique of the sex/gender distinction, Moira Gatens writes:

> Signification, and its constitutive role in the construction of subjectivity, is curiously absent from the writings of the proponents of degendering. This is likely to be an effect of their implicit commitment to a behaviourist conception of the person and the resultant stress on passive conditioning and socialisation rather than the active process of signification. (1983, 148)

Luce Irigaray and Julia Kristeva, among others, have brought into Anglo-American feminist theory the influence of Lacanian psychoanalysis, with its representation of sexual difference in terms of the significance of "having" or "not having" the phallus. This structuralist background has offered an understanding of the relation of signification to sexuality which has challenged the empiricist perspective of feminist social science.

Psychoanalysis, deconstruction, and genealogy have much to contribute, while at the same time contributing their own hostilities, to this theoretical mix. The "lore of the father" creates breached loyalties, both dual and divided, and real and imagined among feminists caught up in this theoretical moment. Yet the work of psychoanalysis and deconstruction offers more to feminist theory than contestation, and the common feminist criticisms of the work of Lacan and Derrida are not as compelling as may be thought. Among the possibilities for feminist theory using psychoanalysis and deconstruction is the scrutiny of theory as theory, and this inevitably includes scrutinizing feminist theory itself.

Gayatri Spivak has named the project offered to feminism in psychoanalysis and deconstruction as "a kind of epistemological project" (1989, 208). The question of sexual difference, arising as the question of "the feminine," has presented itself within those two theoretical undertakings as an insistent bearer of the production of meaning; for Lacan, as the grounds of signification, for Derrida as the necessary "catachresis" of *différance*. It could be hoped that, through these rivals, feminism may make a further impression on the prepared surfaces of patriarchal theory.

What presents itself as alluring to feminist theory in the "loving" regard of the texts of Lacan and Derrida, as Spivak sees it, is that they analyze identity (human, sexual, logical) as a necessary paradox. Quoting Jacqueline Rose's introduction to her Lacanian book *Sexuality in the Field of Vision*, Spivak writes:

> For Rose, "only the concept of a subjectivity at odds with itself gives back to women the right to an impasse at the point of sexual identity, with no nostalgia whatsoever for its possible or future integration into a norm." This desire for an impasse is not unlike the desire for the abyss or infinite regression for which deconstruction must perpetually account. I do, of course, declare myself bound by that desire. The difference between Rose and myself here is that what she feels is a right to be claimed, I am obliged to recognize as a bind to be watched. (1989, 208)

The pleasure and danger of this unstable desire, the bifurcation this presents, is reproduced in feminist loyalties to Derrida and/or Lacan, and in its aggressions. Spivak speaks of "defending a sort of Derrida against Rose defending a sort of Lacan." What is striking in this almost factionalism, as Spivak goes on to point out, is that the something of Lacan that is attractive to feminists using psychoanalysis is something like the something of Derrida that interests feminists using deconstruction.

> I agree with Rose that "to understand subjectivity, sexual difference and fantasy, in a way that neither entrenches the terms nor denies them, remains a crucial task for today." On these terms, in fact, there is not much difference between how she understands Lacan and how I understand deconstruction. (1989, 208)

Against the inanity of an aestheticized reading of Derrida, Spivak wants to represent deconstruction as a theory of the centered, rather than the decentered, subject—as an account of how that subject maintains its centeredness, at the expense of a differential that is sometimes Woman, but that goes under "other" misnomers. In contrast, Rose seems to accept the academic reading of Derrida, while she wants to disturb the self-certainty of a politics, Marxist or liberal, that claims to know the real, the event, and the material ab initio, through the Lacanian account of how the reality of subjects is structured. Curiously, she finds in Derrida only "an endless dispersal of subjectivity" (1986, 20) and asks a question of Derrida that he himself might put: whether only the institution that knows the necessity and impossibility of its limits could be the site of politics. In a later paper she characterizes the problem with Derrida as one of "the absorption of the political (feminist) into the space of representation (feminine)" (1989, 37), which puts Derrida preemptively into an opposition he could be used to critique.

Ellie Ragland Sullivan, another Lacanian feminist, gives Derrida even less: reacting to the criticism of French feminists that Lacan is phallocentric, she opposes a "deconstructive" sort of Lacan to a "psychoanalytic" sort and commends the latter for detailing a material view of language (1989, 64). But this opposition is not convincing, for Derrida, too, reads psychoanalysis. Perhaps the defenses are consequent upon Derrida's own sharp criticism of Lacan, but the feminist reader of Derrida and Lacan need not be satisfied with taking sides.

THE PASSION OF THE SIGNIFIER

The unconscious, "structured like a language," that is, ordered through differences, nevertheless incorporates that order at the level of the body. What else is hysteria, but the exhibiting of the body as a place of signification? This embodiment subverts the neat binarism of the real as against the representation of it. But psychoanalysis is more often read, and not only by feminists, in relation to its signified rather than its signifiers.

In Lacan's "Encore" seminars, Lacan argues there is no sexual relation, since a man only ever sees a woman as the fantasy satisfaction of his own loss, the lack that initiated desire (Mitchell and Rose 1982, 137–61). She represents the phallus for him. Her own jouissance remains outside this fantasy, which nevertheless is all that is known, in the sense that something must be represented in order to be knowledge. Thus, Lacan can say, "There is no such thing as The Woman," by which he means the category of The Woman is a male fantasy, and also that "there is woman only as excluded by the nature of things which is the nature of words" (Mitchell and Rose 1982, 144).

Lacan insists that nothing of Freud's twin insight of the unconscious and infantile sexuality implies a normative theory of mental development or lays down a blueprint against which a life should be judged (Lacan 1977a, 226–32). In his theory of sexuality, Freud freed the sexual instinct from a reductive biological givenness and opened it up to social construction. (I discuss this in detail in chapter 4 of *Passion in Theory*). Psychoanalysis as a science, in his conception of it, took as its scientific object the laws of the unconscious, and provided explanations of its operations in those terms. This rigor insisted on the possibility of a psychical, or ideational, explanation of psychical development, and it lay behind his increasing emphasis on the role of the castration complex in bringing about masculinity and femininity. While always leaving the door open to "constitution," Freud did not resort to the reduction of this development to the anatomical sex of birth. In this he was aided by the insight that the anatomical definition of sex is curiously equivocal.

As Freud notes in a footnote: "[T]he exclusive sexual interest felt by men for women is also a problem that needs elucidating and is not a self evident fact based upon an attraction that is ultimately of a chemical nature" (Freud 1905, 146). The subject of feminine sexuality was destined to lead to argument since, among those embarked on the adventure of the new science of psychoanalysis, not one could lay claim to the objectivity of an observer on questions of sexual difference. By 1933, the argument became sufficiently exemplary as to be referred to as "the debate on female sexuality" among Abraham, Horney, Jones, Deutsche, Klein, and others. This debate has received detailed discussion by Jean Strouse (1985) and Juliet Mitchell, among others—see her introduction to *Feminine Sexuality*, for example (Mitchell and Rose 1982). And the Oedipus complex, in particular, has been examined not as fact, but as narrative, of science by feminist readers. Its "prequel" can be found in the riddle of the Sphinx, which Freud draws on in the *Three Essays* to introduce the child's sexual researches. As Teresa de Lauretis points out in *Desire in Narrative*, that riddle can be read in different ways (1984, 157).

Freud's determination to postulate psychical causes, to be explicated according to the clinical observation of primary thought processes in the unconscious, led him out onto the scene of culture. But he did not leave biology and anatomy behind; the grounding of the psyche in bodily pleasure meant that psychoanalysis continually affirmed the material nature of that scene. That materiality is exemplified in the significance given to the fear of castration that, in Freud and Lacan, is dramatized on the body in a literalizing of meaning, the biblical "word made flesh."

It is as a theoretical consequence of the emphasis on the psychical importance of the threat of castration that the problem of femininity grows. Perceiving castration to be an "accomplished fact" in girls, Freud notes: "The fear of castration being thus excluded in the little girl, a powerful motive also drops out . . . for the breaking off of the infantile genital organization" (1924, 178). The more he is able to explain male sexuality, the less he can account for female sexuality. Freud solves the problem for his theory by "recognizing" that "[t]he little girl is a little man!" Children of both sexes love their mothers first, and the castration complex drives them both out of the phallic phase, the boy in fear, the girl in disappointment and disgust.

But it is ironic that Freud should conclude that the little girl is a little man, since what he set out to account for was sexual difference. The outcome of Freud's sexual research is that he is left unable to answer the question "What does a woman want?" from within his theory. This is an interesting failure in a theory built on the hypothesized sexual wishes of female hysterics. Perhaps in taking desire as the object of its investigation, the science of psychoanalysis guaranteed that its paradoxes would be fruitful.

Feminine desire emerges as a symptom, not only on the theory, but of the theory, that is, it remains the sticking point, repressed and unconscious to put it in terms the theory itself proposes. Psychoanalysis demonstrates something, not merely about desire, but also something about theory. It exhibits how the premises of its explanation (the terms of its observation) are returned to it in its conclusions: beginning from a sexual indifference, Freud is presented with sexual difference as a conundrum. And, as Irigaray's work shows, it provides not only the tools for a feminist analysis, but also its case study.

There is no "fact" that "women do not want," although it may be true that frigidity is not a rare posture for women to take up in relation to the heterosexual act. If the woman is left at the end of Freud's story without any visible desire, it is not because she does not experience it but because his story does not scrutinize the value it gives to paternal authority. It leaves its indelible mark, however, in what Lacan develops as the "Name of the Father," the "paternal metaphor."

Lacan receives Freud's riddle of femininity, and returns it in the form of a love letter. In the later seminars of "Encore," Lacan doubts whether the woman accepts her castration. He notes that there is a great deal left unaccounted for by the notion that the libido is masculine (cf. Freud 1533, 13 1), namely, "the field of all these beings who take on the status of the woman if, indeed, this being takes on anything whatsoever of her fate" (Mitchell and Rose 1982, 151).

The phallus is not an imaginary object (like the breast) nor a fantasy, and "still less" the actual organ. It is a signifier: the signifier of signification as a process: in Rose's translation, it is the signifier intended "to designate as a whole the effects of the signified, inasmuch as it conditions any such effect" (Mitchell and Rose 1982, 80). It stands for the process, and the product, of signification.

In *The Agency of the Letter*, Lacan projects sexual difference onto the Saussurian bar, which he has already inducted into the unconscious as the bar of repression (1977a, 146). The bar is the phallus. It belongs in a dizzy circuitry of metaphor and displacement, which links the notion of the gap needed for signification to the gap required to engender desire. It circulates as the name of the process of representation as such, which makes it the name for that gap; but also as the law that orders repression in order that the subject may represent and be represented, and acquire a sexual identity within a social world; consequently, it is the name of desire, which must be displaced for the subject to do so. The metonymic series of the phallus is as the sign of exchange, sacrifice, and substitution.

This circuitry is what Lacan describes as the passion of the signifier. It unites the word with the flesh, it yokes the material of the body to the structuring of signs: "[H]is nature is woven by effects in which is to be found the structure of language, of which he becomes the material" (Lacan 1977a, 284). This is the strength of the phallus for feminist questions of the place of the body in theory. But the phallus is, all the same, something of a bad dream. It is put together not with the clarity and focus of a theoretical argument, but through a suggestive array of associations, connecting parts of one question to parts of another with apparent profundity. It contains all the astonishment of good metaphor.

Whether Lacan finds the woman's desire to be a man's desire, or whether he finds her specifically feminine pleasure to lie beyond the phallus and therefore outside representation, as the necessary outside of representation, it cannot be said that he has relinquished the patriarchal narrative. We must ask: What joins the phallus to the invisibility of feminine desire? The phallus, Lacan tells us, is the *copula*. The metaphor is a joke, but not less serious for the fact that it disguises itself (as jokes do):

> It can be said that this signifier is chosen because it is the most tangible element in the real of sexual copulation, and also the most symbolic in the literal (typographical) sense of the term since it is equivalent there to the (logical) copula. It might also be said that, by virtue of its turgidity, it is the image of the vital flow as it is transmitted in generation. (287)

He plays on the idea of the copula as that part of speech that links subject with object, producing the relation as such. And the sexual relation reaches its logical expression in copulation, in which Lacan notes the penis is literally the link between two terms. "Typographically," he observes, as if the two lovers lay on the page before us, joined by the erect organ. Lacan then takes the joke to its absurdity, declaring its turgidity to symbolize life. Perhaps at this stage his audience is obliged to drown him out with ribald laughter.

Despite this anonymous joke ("It can be said . . ."; "It might also be said . . ."), this is the proposition Lacan is putting forward. In linking the possibility of representation to the notion of the sexual relation in the copula, Lacan welds the conditions of culture to the function of sexual (in)difference. In the phallus, he represents and disguises the condition of this construction, that is, as an effect of the operation of metaphor. He is helped in this by Freud's preexisting theoretical terms, and by the fact that he repeats a circularity as old as philosophy. If the possibility of human subjectivity is linked by definition to the primacy of the sign of male pleasure, then it surely is an inevitable result that libido will be masculine and that women will lie, inasmuch as they do, outside/beyond the phallus. The phallus presupposes its own "beyond"; Lacan does not escape the logic of his paternal metaphor.

And it must be suspected that he has no intention of escape, for there could be a nostalgic pleasure in this captivity for the male theorist overeducated and ever articulate in coveting the Other in her place, now that she has been guaranteed to remain in it, and even when he knows this desire of the Other is futile avarice. Jane Gallop analyzes this notion of nostalgia in Lacan in *Reading the Phallus* (1985, 146–49). If the feminist reader confronts his desire of her, she discovers that through his courtly gaze, he is looking at his own reflection. He addresses the love letter to himself. His own complaints against the fraud of the sexual relation he distinguishes from those of the feminists, on the basis that "they don't know what they are saying, which is all the difference between them and me" (Mitchell and Rose 1982, 144). Knowledge is a dubious privilege for Lacan, but it is a privilege all the same. Lacan salutes, with his rhetoric, the Freud of an earlier occasion, the occasion of the lecture on "Femininity," where the feminist was informed that her knowledge made her an exception to the class of women, for if she knew better than he, why then, "on that point, you're more masculine than feminine" (Freud 1933, 117).

Luce Irigaray's critique of Freudian theory identifies its emphasis on the acquisition of culture through the masculine position. She argues that Freud sets up a psychosocial inevitability to the acquisition of the law, and thereby the enculturation of the boy, through the threat of castration, but while this logic works very well for the masculine case, in the case of woman the threat has no meaning. Freud thus has no theory for why women come to be in culture at all, and Irigaray identifies his patriarchal assumptions as the origin of his difficulty.

In her introduction to *Feminine Sexuality,* Jacqueline Rose gives a sympathetic summary of what Lacan modifies of Freud's theory of feminine sexuality. She puts Lacan's theory of feminine sexuality into the context of structuralist linguistics, on which it relies, and puts behind the opaque writings of Lacan, as translated in *Encore,* the theoretical context useful for decipherment. It is not that the sign will take its meaning from objects in the world, but rather that signs, in their difference from each other, will delineate a world. The example Lacan gives, of the doors of public conveniences signed as "Ladies" and "Gentlemen," illustrates this graphically, since the "same" object in the world—a door—is delineated by two very different words signifying whole realms of behavior and desire.

Rose outlines three major commitments that Lacan reinforces from Freud, providing a salient summary of the theoretical underpinnings of the theory that emphasises their semiotic bent. "Anatomy is what figures in the account," that is, that anatomy is not destiny, but that this does not mean it does not figure; indeed it indicates that "it *only figures* (it is a sham)" (1982, 44). The phallus "stands at its own expense and any male privilege erected upon it is an imposture." Consequently, "woman is not inferior, she is *subjected*" (ibid.).

Indeed, we may argue that anatomy is itself a metaphor—penis envy seemed to rely on a biological reduction, but for Lacan, the penis is not the point, it is the representation it offers of the body that matters. "The phallus" is a figure, figuring anatomy not as destiny, but as metaphor. Lacan evokes a gendered order in which no one subject has a right, a privilege, or a choice in relation to the other, but rather, an order in which each gendered individual is subjected to an ordering imposed differently on male and female subjects.

Importantly, then, the threat of castration is not the sign of male violence, but of the father's domination, the "law of the father." Obscured in some contemporary feminist thinking, patriarchy is not the relation between the sexes so much as the relation between the father and his progeny; hence, the "name of the father," since one carries one's father's name as a mark of one's identity. The name signifies precisely what promulgates; the father's law.

Male privilege is a fantasy, enacted everywhere; the male position, too, is strictly subject to law, the law of castration. Woman is not inferior but subjected in two senses; to an order that is not her own, but also in that she is made an object for another subject. As with de Beauvoir's philosophy, this postulated relation of Otherness is the source of her difficulty for Lacan.

Although it avoids the worst of biological reductionism, the meaning of the phallus as sign and not as thing does not cure the determinism implicit in the figure. At a certain point, the "symbolic" suffers from the same problem as structuralist theory generally—it is circular:

> It is a strength of the concept of the symbolic that it systematically repudiates any account of sexuality which assumes the pre-given nature of sexual difference. . . . Lacan's use of the symbolic at this stage relied heavily on Lévi-Strauss's notion of kinship in which women are defined as objects of exchange. As such it is open to the same objections as Lévi-Strauss's account in that it presupposes the subordination which it is intended to explain. (45)

The problem for Lacanian structuralism, then, is it does not appear to allow possibilities for meaning to arise outside the symbolic order. The symbolic is self-affirming, and self-referential, even though the meaning allocated to masculine and feminine is "artificial." Kristeva and Irigaray both go "outside" the symbolic in search of other arenas in which meaning might arise, along with women's resistance—the chora, the maternal, and the body. (Bracha Lichtenberg Eittinger, also, uses a notion of the "matrixial" to extend psychoanalytic theory this way.) In his later work, Lacan claims to have a hold of the concept of resistance in the idea of her *jouissance*. However, the concept is never enough to defeat pessimism in Lacan's view on love and the sexual relation, casting Woman as a fantasy in which the masculine subject loses, but never finds, himself. As Rose puts it:

> "There is no sexual relation" because the unconscious divides subjects to and from each other, and because it is the myth of that relation which acts as a barrier against the

> division, setting up a unity through which this division is persistently disavowed. (46)

Love is a disavowal, since it affirms what it denies in "the very ideology of oneness and completion which, for Lacan, closes off the gap of human desire" (ibid.).

The sexual relation is one the male subject has with himself, via the object of the woman, and it never touches the other. The notion of *jouissance*, the excess of meaning, was an attempt to open up the site of resistance. But the problem for Lacan is that because of this view in which meaning is self-referential, he cannot conceive the intimacy of contact with the other; but only ever finds the other as an object presenting itself for exchange rather than as transformation. He tends to blame love for this, but in truth it may be the theory. Indeed, it may be as a consequence of the very figure of the copula, which he assumes. Within the copulative logic, the subject is only ever a subject in relation to its objects; the subject can never encounter the truly other (even while, with deference to Levinas, being might find itself in proximity). The subject *qua subject* is hermetically sealed. (And cf. Olkowski's discussion of Deleuze's subversion of Lacan and the symbolic [1999, 162–67].)

Meanwhile, women cannot be found there at all, or in fact can be found as "not all"—what she is can only be found in what of her exceeds the symbolic grasp of her, that is, her excess, her *jouissance*, her ecstasy. The woman may not accede to her place as object but is unable to assume another, since she cannot "find the words"—the feminine subject would be an oxymoron. The idea of woman is as "not-all," since she is a speaking subject only through mimicry of the masculine. Lacan cannot think the subject except as a position in fantasy; the subject/ object configuration is a fantasmatic structure, and the production of meaning happens only within that fantasy.

Why, then, is Lacan a source of inspiration to some feminism, when he has such a negative and exclusionary view of feminine sexuality? Many theorists have found in there being "things only insofar as there is the nature of words" the chance to reorganize meaning, and redistribute the contrasts between "masculine" and "feminine" through the anatomical sign/ figure/ metaphor. Written on the body, such meanings might all the same be changed. To do so would "modify the moorings that anchor his being," to quote Lacan (1977a, 174), and this ontological possibility has excited some feminist thinkers. The formation of symbolic meaning through the *figure* of the body is better able to be drawn on as opposed to empirical meaning, relating to a fact of the matter, in psychology and sociology, which merely maps people's context. Being and identity, as produced out of a particular set of experiences given to particular (gendered) bodies, gives Freud and Lacan their strength for feminist theory.

Through the concept of the "gaze," Lacan describes the process by which one assumes one's identity for the other. But the identification is always "mistaken," in the sense that an image is taken for the actual existent. The mirror stage essay famously outlines this in the icon of the virtual—the infant makes a first attempt at self-recognition by seeing itself in the mirror. Thereafter, the psychic life of the infant will be made possible, but always mistaken, through the substitution of sign for reality. This concept of an identification that is as much a misidentification helps to explain anomalies in a subject position, at odds with the actual body. Indeed, the body more usually serving as the template of the *imago* is the maternal one. The concept of identification becomes important in Judith Butler's work, helping to explain how one can take on ideas of oneself, including the idea that one can be a subject at all.

DESIRE FOR RECOGNITION

Lacan draws his analysis of the subject partly from Hegel, and it is arguably the Hegelianism in his theory that produces its self-referential effects. But whereas desire for Freud and Lacan remains founded in the sexed body, Hegelian desire, as Rosalyn Diprose (1992) has argued, is an ideal construct on an undifferentiated body. This has created lacunae for feminists using dialectical methods to approach the question of sexed subjectivity, as, for example, in Jessica Benjamin's work, which makes use of the subject/object distinction in a feminist psychoanalysis based in object relations theory. The oedipal is replaced with a notion of the intersubjective, reflecting explicitly on the Hegelian portrayal of the subject's encounter with others in the master/slave dialectic. The links between the social and the psychical are foregrounded, but psychical sexual difference is obscured.

Benjamin writes, in *The Bonds of Love*, in which she considers the configuration of female masochism:

> Conceived in terms of two selves who both wish to be absolute, the father-son struggle does not allow for the recognition of someone outside the self, since the son is constantly taking the father inside himself, trying to become him. The father-son relationship, like the master-slave relationship, is

> a model in which the opposition between self and other can only reverse—one is always up and the other down, one is doer and the other done-to.
>
> This reversible complementarity is the basic pattern of domination, and it is set in motion by the denial of recognition to the original other, the mother who is reduced to object. (1988, 220)

Collapsing the sexual distinction into the distinction between subject and object, Benjamin argues that

> the resulting structure of subject and object (gender polarity) thoroughly permeates our social relations, our ways of knowing, our efforts to transform and control the world; and it is this gendered logic which ultimately forecloses on the intersubjective realm—that space in which the mutual recognition of subjects can compete with the reversible relationship of domination.

In effect, the claim is that gender inequality arises from the refusal to recognize the maternal as a kind of subject—there is no "other" in the dialectic she invokes. However, "if the mutual recognition of subjects can compete with the reversible relationship of domination," it is because of the common conceptual paradox that produces them: the other is, *and is more than,* my object. The other is my *sign.* I, too, must "be a sign for another subject," to be myself a subject, as Lacan observes. Thus, "the mutual recognition of subjects" is not as benign nor as resolved a posture as it seems, entailing the continuing tension of ambivalence. This ambivalence Lacan captures in the other sense of the word *subject,* in which one is "subjected to language," for example.

The intersubjective realm, then, is strictly a realm of signification, on his view. But Benjamin and others following "object relations," assuming that subjecthood is an unambivalent plenitude, can find an implausible idealism in the intersubjective, and can even direct a politics to its attainment.

Lacan is half-persuaded by the fight to the death Hegel imagines from this struggle for the subject position. This Hegel himself describes in *The Phenomenology of Spirit*:

> But the life of Spirit is not the life that shrinks from death and keeps itself untouched by devastation, but rather the life that endures it and maintains itself in it. It wins its truth only

> when, in utter dismemberment, it finds itself. It is this power, not as something positive, which closes its eyes to the negative, as when we say of something that it is nothing or it is false, and then, having done with it, turn away and pass on to something else; on the contrary, Spirit is this power only by looking the negative in the face, and tarrying with it. (1977, 19)

But where Hegel sources the achievement of subjectivity in this aggression, and finds there a generative power for the dialectic—"This tarrying with the negative is the magical power that converts it into being"—Lacan displaces the founding formula onto the Other, the network of signifiers that, as law, generate the possibility of distinguishing anything. This law is called paternal, and it is precisely this oedipal autocracy that presumably Benjamin seeks to avoid.

However, postulating a suppressed maternal position as the cure to the face-off may not fare better for establishing a basis for a genuine relation between the sexes. The mutual recognition forced on the slave by the contest with the master contains a sexual *in*difference in that the subjects are "equal and opposing." While violence is explicated, in this contest for dominance, love, or the need of the other—that recognition of lack that underpins all signification—remains obscure on this position. It has the curious effect of turning a discussion of sexual slavery into a violent confrontation without any erotic color.

Benjamin warns us that

> the intersubjective model of self and other is abstracted from the web of intrapsychic life, which has stamped the history of the individual and the culture with its symbols and fantasies, its drama of subject and object. I have condensed the intrapsychic side of the story as the splitting of tension into complementary forms: subject and object, idealization and repudiation, good and bad, doer and done-to. But my point is that it is crucial to respect the different realities that intersubjective and intrapsychic theory describe, and not to see one as epiphenomenal and the other as essential. (1988, 221)

Funnily enough, this rejection of the priority of either aspect makes her own assumption of a founding character for gender difference in the history of infancy, "the original other, the mother . . . ," not sustainable. But this argument has been also leveled at Lacan's phallus—proposing any origin whether it be paternal or maternal, the law of the father or the ground of the mother, reduces the ambivalence of subject's predicament, as "sign for another subject." Any origin remains fantasied.

Slavoj Zizek engages astutely with the Hegelian elements in the Lacanian account when he reflects:

> Of what . . . does this ontological uncertainty of the subject consist? The key to it is provided by the link between anxiety and the desire of the Other: anxiety is aroused by the desire of the Other in the sense that "I do not know what *object a* I am for the desire of the Other." . . . The core of anxiety is this absolute uncertainty as to what I am: "I do not know what I am (for the Other, since I am what I am only for the Other)." (2000, 71)

Rather than resolving the tension in the mutual recognition of subjects as subjects, as Benjamin does, which has the effect only of shoring up the subject/object distinction, Zizek teases out the incoherence that dissipates it for Lacan, in the postulate of the Other.

> This uncertainty *defines* the subject: the subject "is" only as a "crack in the substance," only insofar as his status in the Other oscillates. And the position of the masochist pervert is ultimately an attempt to elude this uncertainty, which is why it involves the loss of the status of the subject, i.e. the radical self-objectivization: the pervert *knows what he is for the Other*, since he posits himself as the object-instrument of the Other's *jouissance.* (2000, 1)

This demonstrates a more general effect of subjectivity, which Hegel's master/slave portrays; "the satisfaction of a need is subordinated to the demand of the Other" *in order for it to be accomplished* (72), and: "In short, we satisfy our needs in order to earn our place in the social order." The contribution of sexuality to sociality is in this manner installed as a mechanism of the psychical function, rather than left to find itself in an idealized "intersubjective" realm.

BETWEEN THE LEGS OF WOMAN

Lacan can be read and criticized not so much for his slander of his signified, women, but for exposing his metaphysical extemporizing on the Other and its signifiers, and borrowing her illicit pleasure for his rhetorical force. According to Lacan, it can be said that there is a feminine desire: "There is a *jouissance* proper to her, to this 'her' which does not exist and which signifies nothing. There is a *jouissance* proper to her and of which she herself may know nothing, except that she experiences it." The absurd silence of The Woman betrays it as a metaphysical operator, a signifier of what the theory has repressed. Identifying the effects of signification within his theory means we can observe not so much that he was "wrong about women" but that the way in which he offends enables a diagnosis of other parts of the theory (for example, it throws new light on the central role given to castration) and allows us to give more and less to Lacan's theoretical ingenuity. Luce Irigaray offers critiques of this kind of Freud and Lacan (1985a; 1985b).

It is in the theoretical work of Derrida that we find the analytical means to put the question: What is the effect of representing theory (feminist, psychoanalytic) in these metaphysical terms? This I take to be a similar project to that which Spivak identifies as "epistemological" in Derrida/Lacan. One can no more accept the phallus as a state of affairs than one could accept the fact of an Oedipus complex or that the body lay outside theory. The phallus remains an overbearing metaphor; the signifier of signifiers, the paternal metaphor as the father of all metaphor, the metaphor of metaphor as such. In *White Mythology* (Derrida 1982, 207), Derrida argues that the metaphor of metaphor is a general impossibility.

The theoretical task set in deconstruction is to examine the effects of signification in theory; that is, theorizing the "theoretical signifier," and the place of metaphor, model, distinction, and exclusion in the signified it conditions. This project may inevitably appear more artful than one that proceeds from a seemingly self-evident signified (for example, feminism or psychoanalysis). And yet deconstruction is not itself the cause of the instability of certain "scientific" objects of discourse—that "woman" should meet "man," or that "madness" confront "normality" is not attributable to Derrida, but is analyzable as a product of certain originating distinctions. The "real world" (including the body) is not absent from Derrida's critiques, but it does not endure the reflexive nature of deconstruction to emerge as a "beyond" or an "outside" of the circumstances of its representation.

Derrida's work is sensitive to the material effects of discourse; for example, to the real world of cultural exploitation that is consequent upon an anthropology of the West, which is in turn part of an influential metaphysics (see for example *The Ends of Man*, Derrida 1982). Any appeal to the real remains a signification; the challenge is to understand with what it will be answered in consequence of how it has been framed.

Psychoanalysis has contributed both material and method to Derrida's deconstructions of a "metaphysics of presence." Arguing with psychoanalytic theory has been creative for deconstruction, both because a structuralist reading of Freud has been influential in French theory, and because, as theory, the effect of its signifiers on its signified has been fruitfully in evidence. In *Freud and the Scene of Writing* (1978) Derrida traces in Freud's writing the history of his theoretical responses to a perceived real that, as it is named and defined, reemerges conditioned by that naming and definition.

Lacan's "phallus" also provides a deconstructive opportunity. In *The Double Session,* Derrida argues that castration "can never become an originary, central, or ultimate signified, the place proper to truth," because there is no place proper to truth (1981, 268). The term *dissemination* answers the "phallus" by representing "the always already divided generation of meaning." "Dissemination spills it in advance" (ibid.). In *Le Facteur de la Verité,* Derrida scorns Lacan for finding the truth of meaning "between the legs of woman" (1987, 444). Revealed truth, or even a "negative theology" in which truth is seen as reducible to the veil, and to the presence of self-revelation in speech (as in analysis)—these, condensed in the totem of phallus, offend the more fastidious deconstructionist. At stake is the possibility of there being any primary category, or ontological priority: the phallus is a piece of metaphysics that makes the "signifier" itself into a sign of closure. This is why Derrida warns against Lacan, "the purveyor of truth." His caution is repaid by the persistence of the enigma of feminine desire in Lacanian theory, a symptom of its failure to avoid metaphysics.

The piquancy of Derrida's engagement with Lacan, in *Le Facteur de la Verité* and in *Positions,* calls for careful reading, but also illustrates how singular are the steps of the partners to this elegant dance. Derrida finds Lacan guilty of "reappropriation" of some of his own concerns (1981, 107), but nevertheless, he grants to Lacan a historical necessity for his project in postwar psychoanalysis that is not Derrida's own problematic ("this is Lacan's argument" [110]). And at the time of the interview (1981), Derrida allows that his own work might "encounter Lacan's and Lacan's—I do not at all reject the idea—more than any other today" (111).

Derrida will not, however, allow Lacan his eclectic borrowing, from Hegel, Heidegger, and others, when these borrowings remain credulous to the discursive systems in which they arise. He also reserves a suspicion that Lacan's style is an art of evasion. "The vivacity of ellipsis too often seemed to me to serve as an avoidance or an envelopment of diverse problems" (110). And yet: "Perhaps this is a necessary moment in the preparation of a new problematic, provided that the evasion does not speculate too much, and that one not allow oneself to be captivated by the sumptuous representation of the procession and the parade" (ibid.).

Feminist criticism of Freudian/Lacanian theory often refers to a "determinism" in the psychological development of men and women, since it is tied to the bodily difference between them. This assumes that the effects of bodily difference remain static across history, but although Freud may assent to the universality of the Oedipus complex, it is not a logical implication of psychoanalytic theory that the crisis of sexual difference be fixed. Indeed, it is an important consequence of Lacan's thinking through of signification and the unconscious in *The Agency of the Letter* that this not be so; "[T]he slightest alteration between man and the signifier . . . changes the whole course of history by modifying the moorings that anchor his being" (1977a, 174).

On the other hand, Derridean theory is accused of addressing a mere "play of signs," unconnected with the "material world," which designates, on closer inspection of the argument, a world of political action. Both strands of argument are inadequate to the critical task, since they work on assumptions feminism inherits from a model of politics that opposes the base to the superstructure, the economic to the ideological, the material to the representational. Neither Lacan nor Derrida subscribe to these naturalized dichotomies; consequently they cannot be opposed around the question of materiality. Among Derrida's debts to psychoanalysis (possibly even to Lacan) is the recognition of a materiality to language (Ragland Sullivan's distinction between "psychoanalytic" and "deconstructive" based on this perception does not do justice to Derridean ideas of language). Nor, conversely, can Derrida and Lacan be contrasted around an awareness of the signifying quality of the material world; the phallus, for example, is the male organ as it signifies and it does literally in sexual distinction, it being the very organ that makes the difference.

The point of Lacanian desire has been to offer up the paradox of the signifying materiality, and there is nothing "outside" that meaningful matter; there is only the "missed encounter" with what Lacan calls the Real (1977b, 53–66). The resistance of that encounter is analogous, within the limits of its dissimilar context, to the intuition of *différance*, and indeed in Lacan's discussions of the transference, the psychoanalytic concept of resistance emerges as the "rim" of meaning, the moment at which meaning is produced and also threatened. Without the passion of the signifier, deconstruction becomes a theory disembodied, deprived of its material significance. And yet, psychoanalysis as theory belongs itself to the "history of metaphysics," and it can be asked: "[I]n what ways would the Freudian concepts of writing and trace (and, we might add, the Lacanian concept of desire) still be threatened by metaphysics and positivism?" (Derrida 1978, 197).

The proximity between Lacanian law and desire and Derridean presence and *différance* is too sensitive to gloss. The antagonistic extremes call upon both sets of theory to decipher the aggressivity of love (as proposed by Lacan), the complicity of opposition (analyzed by Derrida). The difference might be said to be in the succession, in that deconstruction puts the "next question," the question that follows from the naming of law and desire, which is the question of naming. But given Derrida's testimony in *Positions*, as to the chronology of their writing and reading of certain texts, the question is also one of who succeeds whom, the origin of theoretical debts and the debts of their originality.

The quarrel is "between men." But it should disturb the feminist reader, having profited from the "missed encounters" of Lacan with sexual difference, as well as from the therapeutic action of Derrida's reflections on meaning as such, to overhear that passing shot, "the truth of meaning between the legs of woman." Is a similar move involved in the possibility of feminism? As Elizabeth Grosz (1990) has noted, the conceptual project of any feminism seems incoherent without a definition of woman.

The challenge that deconstruction puts to feminism is to show cause why it is not a condition of its theory that the truth of sexual difference be declared found. And the question is not discredited by feminist criticisms (however justified) that the figure of woman is being used to avoid the real-life variety (see, for example, Braidotti 1989). It remains a question for feminism as to how to relate the figure of woman to the lived experience of womanhood.

Feminist theory faces the question of its own discourse; but will the shift of focus from "signified" to "signifier" (this being the first of two necessary deconstructive moves that would reverse and in that action displace this opposition) threaten the feminist project as politics? On the contrary; how can any politics predict the effects of intervention unless it accounts for change in theory and practice? The body is both real and represented and the difference between bodies is also real and an effect of representations that recognize it as a difference. In short, the body operates in theory both as signified and signifier, the distinction producing its *différance*.

Feminist theory itself has had considerable material effects. "The dance changes place," writes Derrida, in *Choreographies*, "and above all changes places" (1985, 169). There he also writes of the possibility of a "completely other history... of unheard-of and incalculable sexual differences" (167), suggesting that elsewhere in other times and places (such as tomorrow), the kinds of bodies identified as women will find themselves in a different relation to the bodies called men and will demand something different of them, and of each other. Isn't this happening today?

SEVEN

The Figure of the Copula

Moira Gatens critiques the sex/gender distinction as a distinction that elides the sexed body and sexual difference by its separation of biological and social reality. She argues that the distinction does not serve contemporary feminist interests since it eradicates an understanding of the body that is paradoxically required to advance its cause.

Not only does it neutralize sexual difference, but it lends itself to accounts of gender that reduce the sexual politics of gender difference and posit as primary "the relations obtaining between gender and power, gender and discourse, or gender and class—as if women's bodies and the representation and control of women's *bodies* were not a crucial stake in these struggles" (1983, 17).

In the wake of this kind of critique, Judith Butler's work shows how the logic of deconstruction and the politics of genealogy can come together in the analysis of sex and sexuality. Although *Gender Trouble* was published first, its question—whether feminism can have a stable object—is in many ways a consequence of Judith Butler's later theory, developed in *Bodies That Matter,* of how sex is produced.

In *Gender Trouble* the question is posed whether feminism can have a stable object; or whether the notion of woman is constructed by the various social discourses surrounding her, and in particular, by feminist discourse. The answer to the question is offered in the negative: feminism does *not* have a stable object, "woman" is a discourse in relation to other discourses, and it is through discourse that gender is produced.

> By conforming to a requirement of representational politics that feminism articulate a stable subject, feminism thus opens itself to charges of gross misrepresentation . . . the political task is not to refuse representational politics—as if we could. The juridical structures of language and politics constitute the contemporary field of power; hence, there is no position outside this field, but only a critical genealogy of its own legitimating practices . . . the task is to formulate within this constituted frame a critique of the categories of identity that contemporary juridical structures engender, naturalize, and immobilize. (1990, 4–5)

Reading Foucault might lead us to suspect that feminist knowledge is itself a style of knowledge organized according to a set of power relations. The demand for a unified position in the relation to the gender "woman" is a product of a power regime, and is not a straightforward pursuit of justice. This brings to light the disintegration of a humanist hope and creates a disturbance in a whole political and institutional practice, threatening its ongoing viability. That the feminist cause has suffered in terms of membership is perhaps a proof of this.

Butler argues that it makes no sense to assert the specificity of woman as a stand-alone object, outside other axes of power. She signals a skepticism as to whether the object of feminism preexists its analysis. This is a difficult claim for feminism to accept; the politico-theoretical problem whether there is such a thing as "woman" before feminism invents it. But at the same time, Butler seeks to propose something of which feminism could be the discourse, which would allow one to be feminist and continue to work out feminist theory and action, and to desire feminist outcomes.

Like Gatens, Butler scrutinizes what is at stake for feminism in the question, by recourse to the distinction made in feminist discourse between sex and gender. She concludes that the distinction made in feminist theory between sex and gender is incoherent. This leads her to examine the concept of "sex" more closely. The question becomes one of the "discursive construction" of sex; which is to say, how do bodies come to be made as "transsexual," "homosexual," "masculine," "feminine," etc. Butler undertakes this, not only as a deconstruction of the sex/gender distinction, but through a genealogy of the category "sex" such that gender is possible.

The several axes of power constitute subjects in a shifting pattern which account for the instability of the object of feminism. The consequences are that women are not all or always the same, or equal, not always united in what they need or desire, and sometimes these other axes of power locate them in such a way that they are in conflict.

Butler claims it is incoherent to emphasize the masculine/feminine binary. But even where it sometimes make sense to focus on that particular axis of power, what one really needs to understand is how subjects come to be constituted via all axes, so that we might better understand how being a woman is modulated by being in other positions. Her account envisages subjects created by the intersection of power relations, rather than subjects as biological entities onto which power is superimposed.

The problematic question of the interaction between social construction and biological nature assumes that the material of the body precedes all those power relations that identify. But, following Foucault's thinking on the ways that bodies, ideas, and material circumstances are produced out of flows of power, Butler argues that the production of sex also generates knowledge, including self-knowledge, through which one is required to live. Butler explores the social value of certain bodies—"Which bodies are worthy to live?"—by asking, "Which bodies are worth mourning?" in the context of HIV/AIDS, homophobic violence, and more recently, in her discussion of strangers and citizens in a nation at war.

"Sex" comes about in virtue of the shifts in power/truth/knowledge. Butler moves from a conception of the body as an entity on which socialization can take place, to a concept of body which is itself a product of flows of power, identified discursively according to class, race, ethnicity, gender, etc. In this light, she challenges the need for feminism to have a fixed object, to be an identity politics, in order to put forward its demands. While other feminists are concerned that in Foucault and poststructuralism "deconstruction" of identity formations undermines political justification, Butler aims to salvage the possibility of political goals and aims in the context of Foucauldian objects and flows of power.

Gender mirrors sex, according to the sex/gender distinction: there is a biological body and the social conditioning of it follows its biological contour. If, for fear of essentialism, gender is theorized using this implicit distinction but proposing gender as radically independent of sex—as in much empiricist-feminism, when one demotes the importance of the biological and promotes constructivism as the whole account—then gender becomes a "free-floating artifice" in which a *male* body might just as well be described as feminine.

Butler intervenes: "[G]ender is not to culture as sex is to nature; gender is also the discursive/cultural means by which 'sexed nature' or 'natural sex' is produced and established as 'prediscursive," prior to culture, a politically neutral surface *on which* culture acts" (7). This is an effective deconstruction: what was sex, on which gender relies, becomes gender dictating what sex will be—the *reductio ad absurdum.* The logic of oppositions depicts gender as derivative on sex, since sex is designated as the primary and prediscursive term. But in effect, gender as a category is the production of the discursive elements that code sex as prediscursive. The reversal is unconvincing and displaces the naturalism of the binary; Butler reveals the logical operation of the distinction.

In *Bodies That Matter,* Butler achieves a timely synthesis between many elements of poststructuralist theory. Linking the concept of "performativity" from speech act theory and pragmatism with the concept of "citationality" and "iteration" in Derridean deconstruction, and a "disciplinary power" producing bodies through "regulatory norms," as in Foucault, Butler can describe a process by which the sex of a body is produced by the "assumption" of "sex" as performed by a given body. The norm of sexed embodiment is cited in the given body, taking on the marks of it. This "assumption" is the taking on of sexual identity, along with the incitement to do so: gender is conceived as a series of signs emitted by bodies which are both taken on as representative of their identity and/or signal that to other bodies. Clothes, lipstick, hair color, a kind of walk, "throwing like a girl" —the body, not the mind, is taken to be the site of subjectivity. Butler brings together the collected wisdom of psychoanalysis, deconstruction, and genealogy—and its founding phenomenology—to outline the process by which are produced "bodies that matter."

> [T]he agency denoted by the performativity of "sex" will be directly counter to any notion of a voluntarist subject who exists quite apart from the regulatory norms which she/he opposes. The paradox of subjectivation (*assujetissement*) is precisely that the subject who would resist such norms is itself enabled, if not produced, by such norms. Although this constitutive constraint does not foreclose the possibility of agency, it does locate agency as a reiterative or rearticulatory practice, immanent to power, and not a relation of external opposition to power. (1993, 15)

In consequence, "the account of agency conditioned by those very regimes of discourse/power cannot be conflated with voluntarism or individualism, much less with consumerism, and in no way presupposes a choosing subject . . . "

Butler then faces a series of problems, arising from feminist commitments elsewhere—with agency, unity, and democracy as the underlying presuppositions for political action. When asked about the formation of this democratic subject —when asked what democracy would mean for this model of subject-production which is so ambivalent, in the technical sense—Butler has answered: "My view is that the disorientation of the 'I' toward the other would be the very basis of a democratic struggle, which is an open field of discourse of conflict and contestation" (IAPL session, May 30, 2003). This model of democracy is seductive, but does it capture the unconscious of discourse itself, the underside or the "thing" of nationhood, which Zizek eloquently diagnoses? (cf. Butler et al. 2000).

THE LOGIC OF THE COPULA

Feminism is brought to bear on metaphysics through the analysis it makes of difference. In the process, metaphysics is brought to bear on feminism. As *logical* difference, the concept of difference takes part in the logic of identity, which marks out being by distinguishing that which it is not. But as *sexual* difference, the effect of distinction in practice has given rise to subordination and oppression.

There is an isomorphism observable between logic, grammar, the erotic, and the social expressed in the figure of the copula. Study of the copula reveals that this isomorphism is possible since the copula expresses the *making of identity in relation.* The copula names the process of distinction, and names it as generative, as well as hinting at a sexual origin. It generates the conjunction of the sexual and the logical, in one concept; a figure that can bring together the real world and the world of theory; or, in other terms, the conjunction of being and the sign.

The connection between pieces of grammar in the verb *to be* and sexual union can be found in the dictionary definition:

> **copula**, n. (Logic, Gram.) verb *be* (as mere sign of predication);
>
> **copulation**, n. sexual union; grammatical or logical connexion.
>
> **copulative**, Serving to connect; (Gram.) connecting words or clauses that are connected in sense, also connecting subject and predicate; relating to sexual union . . . (*Oxford Concise English Dictionary,* 270)

Benveniste makes the distinction between two uses of the verb *to be,* the nominative and the copulative. One represents the notion of identity as equivalence—for example, "he is Pierre"—and the other contains the notion of predicating—any sentence of the form "this is a that." In the paper *The Linguistic Functions of To Be and To Have,* Benveniste suggests that:

> What matters is to see clearly that there is no connection, either by nature or by necessity, between the verbal notion of "to exist, to be really there" and the function of the "copula". . . . The two have co-existed and will always be able to coexist since they are completely different. But in many languages they have merged. (164)

This is the case in English, for example, where the same word is used for both ideas, both relations. In French, too, "*Etre* establishes an intrinsic relationship of equivalence between the two terms which it joins . . . ," in contrast to the verb *to have,* which performs differently. By contrast, in some non-European languages, the copula need not perform the nominative; one can say "I Pierre I," for example, rather than "I am Pierre."

It seems that, since it is not a universal relation, the joining of the two senses marks something characteristic of Western thought and expression. In the case of a grammar, "identity" and "being" are united, perhaps through historical accident, or at least through some kind of contingency, in the same word. It creates a conjunction that we may call "unconscious," symbolic in Lacan's sense in which the signifier contributes an ontological framework to thought. It is only in a functional sense of language that a homonym can be seen "to coexist, since completely different." An account of the unconscious value of signification places more emphasis on the associations between words, regardless of their rational meanings. For example, Freud notes the rhetoric of the Unconscious often makes use of the "closeness" of opposites, since they are very firmly associated in the mind. And Derrida, too, directs us in the rhetoric of philosophy, to the significance of an accidental coincidence such as that in French between "Hegel" and aigle (eagle). They are firmly bound together in association, while at the same time successfully distinguished, by their common sound.

This isomorphism is anticipated and even explained theoretically by a certain view of "the subject" and "language." Barthes writes, in 'Why I Love Benveniste,' that "linguistics is difficult to expound, divided as it is between a necessary specialization and an explosive anthropological project" (19162).

> Benveniste establishes linguistically, i.e., scientifically, the identity of subject and language . . . the subject is not anterior to language; he becomes subject only insofar as he speaks; in short, there is no "subject" (and consequently no "subjectivity"), there are only locutors; moreover—there are only interlocutors . . . the linguistics of interlocution, language, and consequently the whole world, is articulated around this form: *I/you.* (164–66)

The coincidence of grammar, logic, and erotics is not causal; instead, the subject, in the very act of subjectivity, which is to say in the act of locution, cannot avoid expressing identity *in its very claim of relation to the predicate,* in the copula. The expression is associative, and is predetermined to a large extent by the copula form. "The subject issues from his *[sic]* speech, but at the same time, articulates his whole context in which he speaks, to which he is intrinsically related," as Barthes puts it.

It is through the relation of the subject to language proposed by this view that the link can be made between the conceptual process of identity and distinction, and material and political circumstances of self and relations, including erotic ones. It is also the postulate that clarifies the copula as a kind of *technological* thinking, the subject distinguished from its predicate becoming a subject distinct from its objects, and capable of attaching their means to the ends of the subject.

Heidegger formulates the relation of logic to philosophy consistent with his dictum on technology. Writing in *The Metaphysical Foundations of Logic,* he finds that logic in its derivation from the Greek *logos,* captures the idea of "statement" as both utterance and predication. It captures, that is, both the *event* of identity and the *concept* of the relation between two kinds, given in definition: "Such statements express a determining something as something, a *determinatio.* We call this determining thinking. Accordingly, logic, the science of the *logos,* is the science of thinking" (1984, 1).

Heidegger describes in logic the unity of identity and predication that Benveniste observes in relation to grammar:

> Something, a body for example, is determined as something, as for example, heavy. The "relationship," something (asserted) of something, the predication, is at the same time intrinsically related to a being about which a determination is given in these determinations. That about which determinations are made is the being itself.

It is asserted here that there is a connection between the conceptual form an expression takes and the event or contingency of the existence to which it refers. On the role that logic plays in philosophy, Heidegger concludes:

> [D]eterminative thinking, as thinking about beings, brings, in its own way, the being of being to expression. The simple statement "A is b" shows this in the most rudimentary way. . . . The "to be" that appears expressly in the sentence is termed the copula. The fact that determinative thinking is, in its basic form, tied directly to the "is," to being, indicates that there must be a special connection between thought and being. (21)

The Greek *logos* entails the idea of speech but also of statement, and the ambiguity between self-expression, which is there in the idea of utterance, and proposition, which is there in the idea of statement. Logos, or the statement, is a determining, in other words, a judgment. But in its determining of how things are, Heidegger points out that thinking (as determining) is both related to the *subject* as its activity and to the *objects* of its thought in the content of its judgment. This suggests that logic is primarily about relation as such; the relation that holds between subject and predicate-world is expressive of "copulative" thinking.

Logic, Heidegger tells us, is not about particular examples of statement (2). That is, it is not empirical. It concerns itself with statement as such; "Logic pure and simple has for its theme, thinking about x." Perhaps logic is already the understanding of relation, we might say, since thinking itself is a relation. Heidegger puts before the project of relation, however, as its field, the project of being, subordinating logic to philosophy and promoting the "thinking about x" as the thinking of our being, our specifically *human* being. He establishes a connection between the phenomenology of being and the assistance logic provides in articulating and analyzing the comportment of thinking.

This Levinas critiques, in his claim that ethics precedes ontology, that the assuming of relations to the other is the intellectual operation that inaugurates ontology. And, as Derrida (1987) analyzes it, if questioning being were the philosophical task, the role of logic in *questioning the question* emerges as an ambiguous priority. In *Of Spirit: Heidegger and the Question,* he shows that this priority cannot be wholly coherent, but instead is formed in the operation of *questioning* itself.

Therefore, the copula refers to identity in the double sense of what one is; what one is *identified as*, and one's *being that*—what elsewhere in phenomenology is described as *ipseity*. The copula gives a term to a predicate and, in so doing, makes the term something. Despite appearances, entities are not constituted in themselves, since nothing "is" without that it "is that," according to the logic of the copula. In a certain sense, there is no such thing as tautology, for even a statement of identity ("x is x") attributes more to the term than it contained when it stood alone and uncomprehended, by offering it as the possible subject of attribution. This is to offer it as having an identity, as identified, and thereby, as distinguished. It is at this point that something becomes comprehensible by becoming *legible*.

Further, the difference between what a term is and all the terms excluded by its assertion of identity, gives definition to its being. In distinguishing itself, the term shows itself in contrast and it also shows itself to be a creature of contrast. The shadow of contrast indicates that the term must be in a relation with other terms such that it could contrast with them, and so be identified as itself. Yet this difference is not fixed, and known in advance; it emerges at the event of the term being identified as itself.

In deconstruction, Derrida offers a critique of the production of identity in relation, describing a logic in which one term distinguishes itself from the other in terms of what it is not. In this logic, something is lost and/or violated in the process, that is only recaptured (and not recovered) in *différance*, which is the possibility that the distinction could have been made otherwise.

The deconstructive outline of this copulative logic indicates the difficulties inherent in attempts to rescue scientific knowledge for the feminist project. Donna Haraway, for example, seeks a relation between subject and object that would permit the study of the physical and social sciences within a feminist framework more sympathetic to the insights of difference and identity, through the notion of "situated knowledge."

> Situated knowledges require that the object of knowledge be pictured as an actor and agent, not as a screen or a ground or a resource, never finally as slave to the master that closes off the dialectic in his unique agency and his authorship of "objective" knowledge. . . . A corollary of the insistence that ethics and politics covertly or overtly provide the bases for objectivity in the sciences as a heterogeneous whole, and not

> just in the social sciences, is granting the status of agent/actor to the "objects" of the world. (259)

This notion of the actor is a conception of the object in the subject position, but this defies the logic of distinction that opposes these terms as its very mechanism. Reversal does not work to disarm the "power-charged" relations of which Haraway writes. Advocating the reversal of the opposition of subject/object ignores the logic of the copula, which is that it comes as a *device*. Promoting the agency of the object is as poignant as the suggestion that no term has the agency to which the subject aspires.

EXOGAMY AND SEXUAL DIFFERENCE

How profound is this insight, for women, caught up in/as grammar, as another part of speech? "Kinship is to anthropology what logic is to philosophy or the nude is to art" (1967, 10), Robin Fox observes, in his classic *Kinship and Marriage*. And Lévi-Strauss, at the end of his analysis of the effects of marriage on social relations, writes:

> The emergence of symbolic thought must have required that women, like words, should be things that were exchanged. In this new case, indeed, this was the only means of overcoming the contradiction by which the same woman was seen under two incompatible aspects: on the one hand, as the object of personal desire, thus exciting sexual and proprietorial instincts; and, on the other, as the subject of the desire of others, and seen as such, i.e., as the means of binding others through alliance with them. (496)

Susan McKinnon has argued astutely for the capitalist values underlying this supposedly universal story of nature and culture: "Lévi-Strauss's image of culture depends on an enterprising-up of a natural base," she writes.

> [C]onsanguinity and female sexuality are "marketed" into a cultural form of alliance and exchange managed by fathers and brothers. In transforming female sexuality by regulating its distribution and consumption, and by taking speculative risks in the exchange of "scarce products," men claim a patent on kinship as paternal (and fraternal) property and propri-

> ety. Paternity, proprietary rights in the exchange of women, and culture are all but simultaneous and indistinguishable. (2001, 289)

This logic is dramatically evidenced in Bertrand Russell's *Introduction to Mathematical Philosophy*, where in describing the conceptual elements fundamental to abstract thought, the author encounters social relations. On the first page, for example, Russell introduces the logical property of asymmetry:

> Asymmetry, i.e. the property of being incompatible with the converse, is a characteristic of the very greatest interest and importance. In order to develop its functions, we will consider various examples. The relation husband is asymmetrical, and so is the relation wife; i.e. if *a* is husband of *b*, *b* cannot be husband of *a*... (1993, 42)

In one effortless leap, from difference to sexual difference—Russell reaches naturally for examples of social relations, and particularly of kin relations, in this outline of mathematical philosophy for the uninformed. For example, the abstract relation of "the one and the many," is depicted in terms "where these relations can be made to hold between two terms by creating the many as a class of itself, that is, as a family" (45); and "We may call the class of numbers that are less than n the 'proper ancestry' of *n*..."

In previous chapters, Russell considers the concept of "number" and the intellectual achievement that conceives of the world in terms of number. The "mathematizing" of the world, the ability to abstract, is represented as the underpinning of abstract thought about the world—Russell admires the recognition that three trees growing in a field and three fingers are of the same logical order, as a sophisticated intellectual operation, since in life they look nothing alike; they have no phenomenological immediacy. And yet, their ordering brings them closer to each other, conjoined through the idea of ordering—the number three.

Perhaps it is not an accident that the conceptual finds the social relation as its illustration. But in what way does the social relation bear on it? Russell's metaphors overdetermine it to the point of hyperbole. In the discussion, the figure of husband modulates toward the figure of father, and it emerges through this that the importance of uncovering the relation between "the one and the many" seems to dwell on the desire for "proper ancestry." The concept of number, and then of series, is defined on the analogy of succession, ancestry, and parentage—the relation of king, sovereignty, and paternity is here embedded in an attempt to describe logical relation. Russell's examples are almost obsessively of kin relation, and particularly between parents and offspring. The question of identity in ancestry may come down to the question, "Who am I, and (worse) whom have I fathered?" It brings with it related tropes; legitimacy, property, and the law, as Derrida has exploited in his deconstructions of philosophy (see, for example, the essay on *Plato's Pharmacy,* Derrida 1982). The isomorphism between identity expressed as a logical system, and identity expressed as social order, is not a causal connection, but a conceptual repetition of a formal kind.

For Russell, the idea of description is required of a logic: it is the goal of a logic, to offer a description of the way things are. But in description we find a kind of writing; "description" disguises an invention, by which to describe relations is to lay down certain kinds of privileged regularity. The obsession with "description," as an account of the philosophical task, is related to this formal repetition. The task of description is outlined in Heidegger's discussion of the place of logic in philosophy, where the link to this conceptual repetition is emphasized in the joining of the statement or proposition.

Russell's analysis of number, as an intellectual advance by which it became possible to disentangle the values of trees and fingers so that one can distinguish three, illustrates the relation between sign and value. But how can the living being be entangled in the symbolic order? In the notion of marriage as an exchange, through the idea of sexual difference, Lévi-Strauss unites identity with sociality. Lévi-Strauss gives the classical structuralist account of kinship.

While there may be a dream "of a kind of heaven in which one might 'keep to oneself' "—the fantasy of autonomy is a vanishing point for the tension he describes between the individual and the social—"it is always a system of exchange that we find at the origin of rules of marriage." Marriage brings about kinship outside the "biological" family, and is thus posited as the primary method for relatedness among people in a society. The necessity of exchange develops in Lévi-Strauss as the condition of sociality. The rules of exchange are not a product of society, but vice versa; the society is a product of exchange. The marriage relation is therefore archetypal, because it instates the possibility of sociality, and thus of other kinds of exchange.

Writes Butler, criticizing the sense in which a universal sexual difference is posited in Lévi-Strauss and Lacan as the bearer of sociality:

> Thus, when Zizek writes in *Enjoy Your Symptom!* of the lack that inaugurates and defines—negatively—human social re-

> ality, he posits a transcultural structure to social reality that presupposes a sociality based in fictive and idealized kinship positions that presume the heterosexual family as constituting the defining social bond for all humans. (2000, 142)

Suspicious of the universality claimed for the incest taboo, Butler queries

> the very theoretical postulation of the originary trauma presupposes the structuralist theory of kinship and sociality—one which is highly contested by anthropology and sociology alike, and which has diminished relevance for new family formations throughout the globe . . . (2000, 142)

But, while it is hard to read Lacan without the oedipal resonance—the Name of the Father is an explicitly oedipal structure—Lévi-Strauss's own formulations of the patriarchal exchange are more ambiguous. In places, the pattern of exchange is presented as more productive than sacrificial (a line of thought differently pursued in Deleuze and Guattari's *Anti-Oedipus*).

"The prohibition on incest is less a rule prohibiting marriage with the mother, sister or daughter than a rule obliging the mother, sister or daughter to be given to others. It is the supreme rule of the gift" (1983, 481). The incest taboo is "rather than a prohibition on a certain category of persons, they are a prescription directed towards another category . . . there is nothing in the mother, sister or daughter that disqualifies them as such. It is not that there is a biological revulsion. . . . Instead, incest is socially absurd before it is morally culpable" (485).

As an illustration, Lévi-Strauss cites Margaret Mead's record of the native opinion of sleeping with one's sister:

> The informants had difficulty placing themselves in this relation because it was scarcely conceivable. "What? You would like to marry your sister? What's the matter with you, anyway? Don't you want a brother-in-law? Don't you realise that if you marry another man's sister and another man marries your sister, you'll have at least two brothers-in-law, whereas if you marry your own sister, you will have none? With whom will you hunt? With whom will you garden? Whom will you go to visit?"

There is a profit in the exchange.

Perhaps what gives Lévi-Strauss his distinction is that it is his own theory of myth that permits a critique of the oedipal structure; it is a myth not because it is handed down from the mists of the past, but because it expresses without dispelling an important presupposition for intelligibility. "[M]ythical thought always progresses from the awareness of oppositions toward their resolution," he writes (224 [*Structural Study of Myth* in SA.vol. 1]), and "the purpose of myth is to provide a logical model capable of overcoming a contradiction (an impossible achievement if, as it happens, the contradiction is real) . . . "

Myth is as rigorous as science, Lévi-Strauss argues, and it draws on the same human intellectual capacity. The myth exhibits clearly the "primary process" quality of Freud's dream-thoughts (which Lévi-Strauss explicitly likens it to)—the absence of time, the motility of associations, and the proximity of opposites express a proto-logic, and provide a fantasy satisfaction when real satisfaction is impossible.

The contradiction of sexual difference, that which Lévi-Strauss depicts as the difference between woman seen as sign and as value, seems to strengthen his own argument for myth's applicability in the logical order, even while showing his specific version of exogamy to be partial. Lévi-Strauss's theorizing on incest and myth suggest that the question of the origins of the sexual relation is always a mythical question, and that this relation needs a logic that makes contradiction possible. Consequently, Lévi-Strauss's analysis of myth can also be brought to bear on the isomorphism of language and exogamy.

In the myth of the origin of sexual relations, the contradiction between woman "as a sign and as a value," as Lévi-Strauss has it, is mediated by her maternal capacity, for which she is exchanged, and at the same time in which her agency is crucial. "Mother" provides the transition from sign to value. It links man to woman in the maternal, the subject's origin and yet the first object of desire. Looking ahead to the discussion of Benjamin's psychoanalysis (see chapter 8), we can observe that the ambivalence of the maternal might be seen as essential to its structuring role. Thus, it takes a social imaginary from subject to object of exchange—and more obscurely, from "self" to "other," that terrifying transition which makes possible both love, and the annihilation of indifference. The sacred rites, political forms, and technological appendages of marriage are not analogies for psychological agencies, but containers and materials through which the lived reality of sexual difference is produced.

There is an extensive literature on kinship in feminist anthropology, in the work of Marilyn Strathern, Sarah Franklin, and others. Franklin and Susan McKinnon review the recent history of this field of scholarship in the introduction to their useful collection, *Relative Values:Reconfiguring Kinship Studies.*

Classically, feminism has analyzed marriage as oppressive, from the vantage point of the mid-twentieth century, since the narrative of enlightenment and individualism has now produced a dissonance with the traditional notion of "two becoming one" (cf. Stone, 22). But marriage was not always and everywhere the same.

A survey of marriage in late antiquity and medieval times hints at the contingency of Victorian arrangements of marriage. For example, the change from marriage *in manu* to free marriage in late Rome (Herlihy, 9) or the matrilineality of the old Irish marriage arrangement (ibid., 35) attest to historical differences in the position of women in relation to their kin. Not long before the Victorian era of marriage for life, the early modern family has been described as a transient arrangement in which death functioned as efficiently as divorce does today to put an end to alliance (Stone 1977, 46). The long Victorian marriage can be seen as anachronistic; that said, the wife in the legal arrangement of that time is agreed to have been "the closest thing to a slave in civil society" (13). The role of social opinion operated as coercive, to keep couples together, but where that failed, wives were immeasurably worse off than husbands in the wake of separation.

In anthropological discussions of the evolution of the sexual relation, the question of male domination can be traced from the innocence of prehistory to the fall of the present day. Robin Fox writes:

> It is basic to the definition of a mammal that the young are born live and suckled by the mother. What varies is a) the amount of investment the mother herself puts into the offspring beyond the necessary minimum, and b) the degree and nature of the attachment of a male or males to this basic unit (and the relations of the units to each other). (*Conditions of Sexual Evolution,* in Ariès and Beijin 1985, 2)

In *Kinship and Marriage,* Fox proposes four principles by which this potential is organized, from which all known arrangements can be deduced. These are: (1)The women have the children; (2) the men impregnate the women; (3) the men usually exercise control; (4) primary kin do not mate with each other. "Gestation, impregnation, domination and the avoidance of incest, lie at the root of all social organization" (Fox 1967, 31).

Fox sees feminist objections to his principle three as "somehow unreal," given the examples of history. His *explanation* for male domination is a familar one (similar to that used by de Beauvoir, in existential dress and discussed in chapter 1, from *The Second Sex*), viz., that the child handicaps the woman since child rearing is a "highly specialized task," and further, this necessity of maternal attention for the long years of child rearing is "rooted in primate nature."

Even in the realm of the sexual, there is that large part of woman's (physiological) realities which is not captured in her reproductive capacity. One thing on which the anthropologist's argument is notoriously selective is on *what* of biology will be considered determinative. For it is just as true to say of nature that "she" gave intelligence and manual dexterity to both sexes equally, and an equal power of speech, at the same time as was bestowed sexual difference.

But Fox pinpoints the "handicap" to women of childbearing at a precise moment in evolution: with the development of the "hunting ape-man *[sic]*" whose young must now be provisioned with meat (to support the maturation of the larger brain, etc.), rather than left to forage vegetable matter for themselves. The brain, which is both cause and effect of this story, precipitates a sexual division of labor unparalleled in the animal world. In Fox's "narrative reconstruction," vegetarian primates first live as a coalition of the three interest groups, where supply and demand dictates dominance. The situation is not considered from the point of view of the benefit of individual members, that is, their satisfaction, but only from the overall benefit to the group of survival of at least some of them.

But meat added to diet requires hunting, and further, hunting that uses intelligence and tools, since the modification is too rapid for the "ape-man" to have developed "natural weapons." A bigger brain evolves to meet the task. Here, the gap between nature and culture is created, and the evolution of the brain passes over onto the achievement of culture, rather than nature. With the introduction of the ape-man, the narrative perspective has changed from the survival of the group to the agency of the male members of it.

Hunting becomes sexually adaptive from one sex, male, in its quest to attract the other, since the females need to rely on a social context to provision their young for the first time. This marks the entry of the classical myth of "sex selection." But it is not clear why the female kin-groups are not organized as lionesses are to hunt for each other, given that they are presumably provided with the same "bigger" brain.

A sexual division of labor is instituted in which, despite males and females having similar capacities, a pronounced "dimorphism" appears between the sexes, and in which the *males* collaborate in competitive alliance, when previously they had competed only—the appearance of the myth of the primal horde.

Kinship and marriage systems redefine relations between the three interest groups, which are now linked, and at the same time are allocated spouses, according to descent. Exogamy, Fox applauds, is "rightly seen by Lévi-Strauss as a positive system of exchange—that is the truly human innovation"—the entrenchment of a sexual division of labor underwritten by male domination is once again identified as the definitively human (11).

And the evolution of this large brain is credited to the male, who developed it through experience in hunting, for which process the female rewarded him by mating with him. Where were the females, in this "feedback loop" of greater intelligence bringing a larger nutritional yield for the production of intelligence? It is uncanny how this story repeats the metaphysical one in which humanity is a masculine attribute. As Lévi-Strauss writes: "[M]yths get thought in man unbeknownst to him."

Nevertheless, there are some problems with this story: It is circular—the agency of evolution is described as competitive, and an assumption of the value of competition to a proposed "sexual selection" serves to explain a competition *between* the sexes. Competition explains competition. Further, it is circular in describing the agency of *genetics* as a competitive force, only to use genetics to explain the drive in a species toward social competition. Again, competition explains competition. Models of the "truly human," defined as that in which *women* are exchanged, are used to explain how that exchange must have evolved—a social model is projected onto an imagined past and then traced to the present. Thus, the present explains the present.

The explanation is also haunted by other myths—stories of the origin of Man as babe in his mother's arms, and of the social contract, are projected onto species history, so as to explain the coming-about of the social contract. This, too, is circular. But, notably, the story is also haunted by any number of myths about the feminine, from Eve in the Garden of Eden on. Society exists for the sexual appetite of the man in his prime: his potency defines it, and interprets it, too.

Lévi-Strauss criticizes Freud for having located the story of the primal horde, postulated as the prehistory for the Oedipus complex, as a story about origin when it in fact depicts an equilibrium in the present between certain kinds of desire. The story of the primal horde describes not a past conflict but a present one, that will not be enacted in virtue of being symbolized (1969, 492). The same criticism can be made of Fox's analysis, and Lévi-Strauss's own—indeed, the question of sexual relations in contemporary societies is linked to the prehistory of the species only as old myths are related to their more recent versions.

In recovering the repetitions and transformations in the scientific view of kinship and sexual practice of the past and present, one may be struck by how similar these "different" versions are of meaning, which stands in for male domination, expressing this mythic desire. Lévi-Strauss's story of exogamy and exchange are the same myth, one that Freud too told, as that of the "primal horde," and Lacan puts forward as the Name of the Father.

The "human" and "life" sciences in general "act as legitimating meta-languages that produce homologies between social and symbolic systems," Donna Haraway (1991) argues. She makes an influential critique of the primatology that underwrites these stories of sexual difference in the human, in *Simians, Cyborgs and Women*:

> Theories of animal and human society based on sex and reproduction have been powerful in legitimating beliefs in the natural necessity of aggression, competition, and hierarchy. In the 1920s, primate studies began to claim that all primates differ from other mammals in the nature of their reproductive physiology: primates possess the menstrual cycle. That physiology was asserted to be fraught with consequences, often expressed in the fantasy-inspiring "fact" of constant female "receptivity." (22)

The categories of kinship then become the structure through which it is postulated that "culture would then be the logical domination of a necessary but dangerous, instinctual nature."

> . . . [O]ur nature has been theorized and developed through the construction of life science in and for capitalism and patriarchy . . . it is . . . part of the maintenance of domination in the form of escalating logics and technologies of command-control systems fundamental to patriarchy. (68)

This science contaminated with patriarchy raises a difficult question for feminism as she sees it, one she poses as: "How can feminism, a political position about love and power, have anything to do with science as I have described it?" She finds her answer in a theoretical perspective that sees "domination as a derivative of theory, not of nature" (23). "In a strict sense," she writes, "science is our myth" (42). And while it may be that "it is not easy to imagine what evolutionary theory would be like in any language other than classical capitalist political economy" (39), that it is hard to know "what life science would be like if the historical structure of our lives minimized domination," nevertheless, the history of biology would suggest "that basic knowledge would reflect and reproduce the new world, just as it has participated in maintaining an old one" (68).

Donna Haraway's ambivalence about the conceptual relations suggested in kinship are expressed at one time as the desire to be kin to cyborgs, simians, vampires, and the oncomouse, while at another, as being "sick and tired of kinship." In analyzing Haraway's work, Franklin does not blame her for being tired of the nuclear family and its discontents; she only finds her continuing attraction to the kinship model surprising and problematic, given that kinship itself exhibits, in Franklin's estimation, a desire for knowledge of the "good old appropriative capitalist kind." (Franklin and McKinnon 2001, 316).

EROTICISM

According to Lévi-Strauss, the "magic of this dream" of the primal horde—its "power to mold men's thoughts unbeknown to them"—arises precisely from the fact that the incestuous and murderous acts it invokes are not committed. (But Judith Butler asks, in her critique of Lévi-Strauss in *Gender Trouble*, "How do such phantasms become generated and, indeed, instituted as a consequence of their prohibition?") "Because culture has opposed them in all times and all places," the dream remains as the permanent expression of desire for disorder or rather, counter-order. In a similar way, festivals turn social life topsy-turvy, not because life was once a Bacchanalian orgy, "but because it has never been and can never be, any different" (491).

Ambivalence is the difficult companion of identity, emerging with the distinction to put it into question. In virtue of the generation of a term, emerging from that which it is not in its contrast, it is obvious that in a certain sense, there both is, and is not, an "x." Ambivalence measures this; but is not a comfortable, or even a stable, point in the logic of expression. "Contained within the psychic topography of ambivalence, the faded social text requires a different sort of genealogy in the formation of the subject, one which takes into account how what remains unspeakably absent inhabits the psychic voice of the one who remains," writes Butler, specifically of mourning, in the *Psychic Life of Power* (1997, 195).

But, because of the requirement on us to be, to have meaning and to find value, ambivalence as a *psychical* symptom is disconcerting to others. It interrupts relations, and frustrates the reinforcing of bonds and the building of common values. It is not strategic; it speaks to alienation and dissociation, rather than connection and fulfillment. It can only be avoided, however, by a certain fraud, a "blinking" at which we are all necessarily adept. Social relations such as marriage and kin are among the most important in this regard, for overriding the affect of ambivalence driven by the unstable generation of identity, by maintaining structure.

"Survival is a matter of avowing the trace of loss that inaugurates one's own emergence," Butler suggests. The subject, grieving or desiring, "is implicated in a loss of autonomy that is mandated by linguistic and social life; it can never produce itself autonomously" (195).

The figure of the copula dictates that there is a relation between the social-real and the logical-conceptual spheres; it expresses this as a generative one. Indeed, the copula indicates that value can be produced *only in* relation, and that relations of comparison and contrast between terms build a conceptual scheme, and at the same time, an arrangement of values amounting to an ethics. If values were not produced as material events in contrast with other experiences of contrast—as the artist's phrase "color values" attests—then ethics would have no power to trouble us. But the play of contrast and comparison is felt as pleasure and pain, and intimacy functions to join terms in the social equation, in relations with others. The copula expresses a nexus between this pleasure-pain and the conceptual event of value, by adopting the form of both the social subject's predications and the production, through the contrast of identity and negation, of chains of evaluation.

> But woman could never become just a sign and nothing more, since even in a man's world she is still a person, and since in so far as she is defined as a sign she must be recognised as a generator of signs. . . . In contrast to words, which have wholly become signs, woman has remained at once a sign and a value. This explains why the relations between the sexes have preserved that affective richness, ardour and mystery which doubtless originally permeated the entire universe of human communications. (Lévi-Strauss)

The copula not only makes something of its subject, but it makes "her" a "woman." How much of being "the woman" is produced as an experience of being in contrast? The figure of the copula provides more than a rhetorical bridge between philosophy and feminism; it provides a conceptual structure that depicts logical, rhetorical, and material relations. And, while the product of the copula is identity, relation, and distinction, it is significant that the copula's mode is *proximity*. That is, while generative of concepts, the copula is not itself conceptual, let alone propositional. It is eventful and inventive, and its action shapes and forms.

The erotic body, which surrenders itself to the collapse of self-definition in the sexual act, has experienced how acutely the procedure of definition is the condition of psychical identity. As the *Story of O* foretells, this is not a safe place to remain, although a sublime state to pass through. To lose oneself in another can be kin to madness, and in their dedication to love, some subjects appear to contravene the contemporary norm of self-identity. While therapists devote themselves to repairing this "loss of self," which in the modern world looks pathological, at other times it might be speculated that this has been a necessary psychical formation for femininity. The woman "who loves too much," that is, whose identity is porous and diffuse, is a subject "too close" to her predicates, so that she almost cannot distinguish herself from them. But in the traditional fantasy of marriage in which "two become one" it is the feminine identity that is merged (banally shown where she takes his name, or in the designation of the traditional service that pronounces the couple "man and wife").

Bataille (1962) would say this ambivalence is the defining quality of erotic being. In his account of the erotic relation, admiring the expurgating of anxiety about identity through the human or animal sacrifice, he posits the other as the sacrifice made in the performance of subjectivity. Bataille describes the erotic drama of the copula as a drama about continuity and discontinuity of the self, as particularly related to life and death, both as reality and as trope.

> The whole business of eroticism is to strike to the inmost core of the living being, so that the heart stands still. The transition from the normal state to that of erotic desire presupposes a partial dissolution of the person as he exists in the realm of discontinuity. Dissolution—this expression corresponds with dissolute life, the familiar phrase linked with erotic activity. In the process of dissolution, the male partner has generally an active role, while the female partner is passive. The passive, female side is essentially the one that is dissolved as a separate entity. But for the male partner the dissolution of the passive partner means one thing only: it is paving the way for a fusion where both are mingled, attaining at length the same degree of dissolution. The whole

> business of eroticism is to destroy the self-contained character of the participators as they are in their normal lives. (17)

But even in the logic of the copula, it seems that the dissolution of only the female partner will not precipitate the two-become-one, despite the heterosexual fantasy at work in that image. Nor, conversely, could the desire for fusion leave the male identity completely unchanged. In attributing this dissolution to the feminine or passive partner, Bataille documents the literalizing of an "intellectual" fault: observing the other's dissolution as a substitute for one's own is to have both the continuity and the discontinuity in one maneuver. This is classically a *disavowal.*

The imaginative projection onto the feminine role of the dissolution would, as Bataille implies, represent (and replace) death for the subject himself. The aim of the erotic exercise from the point of view of the subject must be more than this dissolution, the subject retaining for himself the *double* movement, in an identity lost in dissolution but projected onto the other, through whom he can experience it while his identity is protected. Logically, the project of fusion is impossible. The idea of two becoming one, which operates for the subject as this disavowal, is the very "fraud" of love, as Bataille calls it—the promise that the other will allow that dissolution of identity by dissolving in one's place. Whereas in reality, as death and as psychosis, the loss of identity may be horrifying.

The law of noncontradiction lies at the heart of the matter, both for logic and for erotics, inasmuch as they are both mimes of identity. Relation is not possible in the radical absence of the other/predicate. The law of noncontradiction is the rule obliged by this project of thinking. The very operation of identity, and the disavowal that must accompany it—denying ambivalence—is *experienced* in the erotic and social relations, and *formalized* in the logical relation.

There is an affinity, then, between definition and separation; repression and disavowal; continuity and discontinuity. Extinguishing the ambivalence of the self-other relation is an intellectual fault, regarding the products of distinction as essentially distinct in their natures. It is strangely contiguous with the depravity of murder, as Bataille theorizes. "Bodies open out to a state of continuity through secret channels that give us a feeling of obscenity. Obscenity is our name for the uneasiness which upsets the physical state associated with self-possession . . ." (Bataille 1962, 17).

The copula goes through the notion of the paternal law and the masculine lover to encounter the instability of definition as such. A necessary disavowal operates in these orders—logical, social, erotic—to support the copula. This entails a projection onto predicates and others, which involves the feminine in its theatre. Thus, between the logician and the pornographer there lies an intellectual affinity. Susan Sontag writes of Bataille's pornographic novel *The Story of the Eye*: "The universe proposed by the pornographic imagination is a total universe. It has the power to ingest and metamorphose and translate all concerns that are fed into it, reducing everything into the one negotiable currency of erotic imperative. All action is conceived of as a set of sexual exchanges . . ."

> Of course the pornographic imagination is hardly the only form of consciousness that proposes a total universe. Another is the type of imagination that has generated modern symbolic logic. In the total universe proposed by the logician's imagination, all statements can be broken down or chewed up to make it possible to rerender them in the form of the logical language. (Sontag: "The Pornographic Imagination," in Bataille, *Story of the Eye,* 112)

The Story of the Eye is the expression of a personal metaphorics, a configuration representing a desire. In an appendix, the metaphors of the eye, the egg and of fluids are related to autobiographical incident. The biography of the author is then offered as that order in which these two chains of metaphor are fused, illustrating that erotic connection is a matter strictly of empirical record. It is in this sense of the empirical that the body is entangled in the symbolic—it is only as a result of the biographical event that the image causes arousal. This is characteristic of the unconscious postulated as "structured like a language," and the erotic provides only a graphic instance of it. As a theoretical result, Barthes writes in *The Metaphor of the Eye*: "*The Story of the Eye* is not a deep work. Everything in it is on the surface . . . it is a case of signification without a thing signified (or in which everything is signified)" (123).

The arbitrary and the necessary meet in this view of the unconscious; the contingency of what particularly and in fact *produces arousal*. Otherwise, it is only at the formal level that admiration for the pornographer is won. As Barthes expresses it, *The Story of the Eye* is "a perfectly spherical metaphor, each of its terms is always the significant of another term (no term being a simple thing signified) without it being possible ever to break the chain" (122). In identifying desire as only ever signification, as exhausted in the event of representation, pornography, like logic, demonstrates the operation of the figurative in identity as such, the "logical fiction" that allows the subject to identify (with) its objects at all.

The subjective impasse that the figure of the copula expresses, between the object and subject relation and its disavowal, is experienced in the erotic relation, and depicted in pornography, while the ambivalence it implies is not yet a thinkable (i.e., logical) space. At the same time, the "end" of metaphysics is proposed, the intensification of technology arises, and even the equality between the sexes, come together in this figure of the copula, as it produces subjects and objects alike. It is possible to argue that in a *technical* sense, the copula is the limit of the known world.

EIGHT

The Body as Material Event

In my previous chapter, I argued that the logic of the copula entails an encounter with philosophy for feminism. But the figure of the copula, in representing the necessity of the body for the mind, also entails a feminist encounter for philosophy. It is through feminist theory that this body is understood not merely as a platform or life-support machine, but as conceptually generative.

One possible theoretical source of feminist understanding, for the origin of the intellectual in the copulative, is the account put forward by Freud of the advent of *thought* in the psyche. It is not an accident that the argument is developed through a discussion of the erotic position of the masochist, for the masochist emerges as the subject who understands through her desire, which is to say through her body, what constitutes the necessity of thought.

It is telling that the nexus of thought and sexuality should lie with the body of the masochist, since the *real* problem that remains for feminism is violence. At its most naive: How can the sexual relation, which is supposedly full of love, be violent? The sexual relation in its resonances and ambiguity, can in no way be confined to love, either heterosexual or homosexual. It cannot be reduced solely to a social relation, because in one of its aspects it addresses the most intimate subjectivity, while in another it is central to our animal embodiment and reproduction.

In a certain feminist lifestyle advocacy, those women who are in same-sex relations avoid sexual violence by avoiding men, and those who are in heterosexual relationships, strive to find the "right kind," that is, relationships of respectful and supportive love, rejecting all signs of aggression—from sexist disparagement and emotional cruelty to sexual humiliation and physical assault—as "abuse."

This dichotomy does not explain the proximity of passion and aggression, Neither in love between men and women or in same-sex relationships between feminist women. As rational counsel, it resists the important sense in which the erotic is, and is even valued as, the excess of the rational. And, as an analysis of the oppression of women it defeats itself, for to insist on masculinity as violence itself, and/or on the sexual relation as properly governed by reason, seems to miss the point of both love and feminism.

And feminisms, which set out to address and redress the oppression of women, have become rivalrous themselves. Are these aggressions a legacy of the intellectual world they must take place in (but if so, why is the academic world so full of passion, when it so thoroughly divorces ideas from affects?). Have we overlooked an aspect of the relation between sisters? Feminism has not addressed the question of aggression in feminism as anything more than contamination.

Perhaps, after all, the thing that feminism has not yet successfully addressed is love. The "battle between the sexes" has not rendered the ambivalence of the sexual relation. As a species of theory, feminism has relished the rigor of distinction and has not found it easy to tolerate the proximity of opposites.

A striking example is the contemporary discursive event of the sexual relation as abuse. Where once a man beating his wife was regarded as an exercise of husbandry, the contemporary scene, which feminism has played a part in shaping, now renders this as "domestic violence" and makes it a crime. For example, in the history of Victorian marriage, it was a long struggle for women to be accorded separate identities from their husbands, and thus for domestic violence to be revealed as a "crime to the person" (Stone 1977 [cf. Love and Marriage, etc.]). This does not solely attest to an enlightenment in the (hetero)sexual relation, despite what we may want to believe. It is plausibly understood against the changed conceptions of subjectivity which today require high levels of psychical separation and physical integrity, to maintain the liberal subject and its necessary postulate of autonomy. This specific bodily aesthetics forms us away from, say, physical expression toward the verbal and propositional.

While physical assault was almost certainly visited on wives in virtue of their subordination to a man (including their economic dependence), nevertheless we cannot assume that the experience of it has been to other women as it is to us today. We cannot assume that a wife experienced herself as separate from her husband in the way that the contemporary subject, man or woman, is formed to do. For the contemporary feminine subject—and especially the feminist subject—sexual assault is a *conceptual* as much as a physical trauma. It is the breaching of a body, which society dictates must remain self-contained to recognize itself. This social requirement of supposed autonomy indeed offers the feminine body *of itself* as the site of a trauma—as a body unable to complete its social reality in the (masculine) norm of autonomy. The addition of violence activates this trauma, and renders it visible.

THE PLEASURE OF THE SLAVE

If however, through identification in the analytic (and psychoanalytic) sense, we take the couple as one unit, not as two, we see a familiar operation of definition and identity; the male term experiencing the ambivalence of its destruction (as a self, as much as a living body) in the pantomime of the figure of the other. As I discussed in the previous chapter, Bataille suggests that this satisfaction can be taken even to the extreme of human sacrifice; retaining the ambivalence in a disavowal by which the male subject experiences the loss of self in his surrogate (woman), while preventing the annihilation of his own subjectivity, a structure that can only be loosened at great psychical peril.

The submission portrayed from the feminine point of view confirms this peril—in the *Story of O*, for example, the loss of self is characterized as a narrative leading to death. It may be no surprise that masochism has offered itself as both a site for the worst of chauvinist fantasies, and a literally perverse space for figuring politically, even in feminist terms, a pleasure beyond prescription.

In analyses of masochism, the masochist's mechanism of satisfaction is usually analyzed as one in which intrapsychical states are projected into the intersubjective realm. Focusing on masochism, not as the pathological actions of the pervert, but as the pleasures of the slave, highlights the subjective experience of a paradox. That paradox is, as Laplanche and Pontalis write, the one that also interested Freud; that there is "a state of affairs that lies at the root of the masochistic perversion and that is also to be found in moral masochism: the fact of sexual pleasure being bound to pain" (Laplanche and Pontalis 1973, 245).

Freud's own account of masochism is outlined in relation to a masochistic fantasy in the essay *A Child Is Being Beaten.* Laplanche and Pontalis's analysis of the concept of fantasy in psychoanalysis serves to explain why this instance of the erotic has conceptual consequences for the relation between mind and body. Their reading of Freud—outlined later in this chapter—is fruitful, because it allows one to address the problematic of going between the psychical and the social not just as the relation between subject and other, but as raising the question of the ontology of *thought* in a theory of the subject.

Jessica Benjamin (1995) makes an explicit claim to "going between" psychoanalysis and feminism in her introduction to *Like Subjects Love Objects.* In *The Bonds of Love,* Benjamin considers masochism and feminine desire for submission through the example of *The Story of O.* The story is considered as a report of a desire; not as a fantasy, nor yet as a text. Benjamin is interested in considering masochistic desire for what it suggests about domination and submission which, she argues, is a real-world configuration that conflates self and other with the gender polarity, having its origins in both the individual's history and the social practice of being mothered.

In this, perhaps, she might be thought to be more feminist than psychoanalytic. Certainly, the analysis she provides of the desire is exclusively in terms of power relations between subjects (pleasure is not the point), simplifying any intrapsychical dynamic to an implicitly Hegelian model of self-consciousness. In effect, this means her analysis of the self/other relation is of the other as ideally "an equivalent centre of consciousness." The uncanny other, the unconscious, and indeed sexuality, is functionally absent.

Benjamin's view of sadomasochism is a dialectical one, as is her "solution" to the problem of domination. It proposes not to deal with the pleasure of the slave, but assumes that if the self was configured "ideally" this pleasure would be replaced by another, that of mutual recognition. In her later book, *Like Subjects Love Objects,* Benjamin embraces this dialectical approach as a psychoanalytic practice:

> [T]he basic formal logic of my argument remains essentially the same as in my earlier work: reintegrating the excluded, negative moment to create a sustained tension rather than an opposition. This logic holds whether we are talking about the relation between self and other that the ideal of masculine rationality and autonomy have excluded, or about the necessity of destruction that the ideal of recognition might exclude. But whereas this logic replicates certain moves elaborated in deconstruction—reversing and elevating the negated element in an opposition—the practice of psychoanalysis pushes toward something rather different. The lost possibili-

> ties of theory have to lead us toward a reconstruction of what we encounter in practice. (23–4)

This "reconstruction" is not a "deconstruction," but not just because theory leaves us too soon, before an encounter in practice. The process described, of "reversing and elevating the negated element in an opposition," is a description of a dialectical, rather than a deconstructive, logic. This has important consequences for the subjectivity Benjamin is diagnosing.

> Deconstruction cannot limit itself or proceed immediately to a neutralization: it must, by means of a double gesture, a double science, a double writing, practice an *overturning* of the classical opposition *and* a general *displacement* of the system. (Derrida 1982, 329)

Benjamin's procedure does not displace the comfort of the two terms in their mutual conceptual dependence. In Derrida's terms, and according to his analysis of Hegel in, for example, "From Restricted to General Economy: A Hegelianism without Reserve" (Derrida 1978), one could say that this reconstruction is too *profitable* to amount to a deconstruction. In the idea of a "mutual recognition," Benjamin recoups the difference negated, and renders it in a common currency. Mutual recognition finds a basis for the other in shared judgment—the return is "with interest," since what was given away in entertaining ambivalence or tension at all, is gathered in again in the comforting possibility of an exchange. The difference between deconstruction and reconstruction would become clearer still in relation to the "intersubjective" thereby proposed, whose norm is often (as Lacan astutely observed of ego-psychology) that of the subject/analyst.

The omission of pleasure from Benjamin's analysis of masochism, despite its model being found in a pornographic narrative, and the absence of sexuality in general from the account, performs a worrying elevation of its own. Rather than going between the psychical and the social, it may take masochism away from the psychical and into the social—there to cauterize its desire?

Rosalyn Diprose has described the Hegelian model of desire, on which Benjamin's view is implicitly predicated, as resulting in an "anti-body" erotics, one that

> begins from the problematic assumption that relations with others are based on objectification and that, through our

> objectification of others and ourselves, either the body reigns as flesh, in which case domination or submission follows, or consciousness puts its body and that of others at a distance, and freedoms are preserved. (84)

She argues that this intersubjective space is posited as a space of consciousness, transcending the passive flesh of the body, which is the "locus of submission." Its surface of sexual indifference masks the familiarity of this view with traditional philosophical accounts of the privilege of the masculine mind/subject over the feminine body/object. This means, in Diprose's estimation, that the feminist analysis "that follows this logic in the interests of promoting women's freedom does not even succeed in its aim of protecting women from domination" (84).

Against the dialectical reading of masochism offered by Benjamin, in which the meaning of masochism is the duality of dominance and submission, Gilles Deleuze suggests, in *Masochism: Coldness and Cruelty,* that sadism and masochism appear symmetrical, not because they are true poles of each other, that is, as the reversible opposition of dominance and submission, but because of their *signifying habit* of transferring the intrapsychical onto the intersubjective. "In place of a dialectic which all too readily perceives the link between opposites, we should aim for a critical and clinical appraisal able to reveal the truly differential mechanisms as well as the artistic originalities," he writes (1989, 14, and cf. Deleuze 1997).

In the case of masochism, the critical has something to teach the clinical about the nature of the sign. In fact, Sade's and Masoch's fantasies raise the issue of the reality of the sign, and here social and psychological theory need the *aesthetic* to properly appreciate the ontology at work in them. The problem for an appeal to the political realities of domination versus recognition such as Benjamin makes is that it forecloses the intricate question of *what is real.*

The problem reconfigured in this way is that while the masochist desires to be dominated, the desire for mutual recognition *also takes place in thought.* Within the medium of thought and fantasy, a masochist *folie-à-deux* or a feminist imagining of mutual recognition are ontologically equivalent, and it becomes a question only of how alone one is in one's fantasy (which is to say, in one's pleasure). In effect, the feminist problem is that they both happen "between" the psychic and the social, and by an apparently unspecified mechanism. What distinguishes a valued desire from a denigrated one, and moreover, what in the subject gives rise to desire at all?

"The status of fantasy cannot be found within the framework of the opposition reality-illusion (imaginary). The notion of *psychical reality* introduces a third category, that of structure" (Burgin 1986, 27), as Laplanche and Pontalis argue of Freud's theory of sexuality.

It is necessary to identify the structure of this "going between," so as to avoid an ontological collapse into the opposition of real and imaginary. In Freud, the structuring effects of psychical reality account for the transition from bodily urge to formulated (even unconsciously formulated) desire. And this interpetation is the "literary" task that Deleuze sets psychoanalysis through the classic masochistic novel, *Venus in Furs.*

Venus in Furs is the story of a sexual relation in which it appears the feminine is dominant. But, despite the infamous contract ("You will renounce your identity completely," etc.) in which Severin abrogates all rights to life and identity to his Venus, it is in fact a production "from the bottom up." Deleuze observes: "The masochistic ego is only apparently crushed by the superego. . . . The weakness of the ego is a strategy by which the masochist manipulates the woman into the ideal state for the performance of the role he has assigned to her" (Deleuze 1989, 124).

> In projecting the superego onto the beating woman, the masochist appears to externalize it merely in order to emphasize its derisory nature and make it serve the ends of the triumphant ego. One could say almost the opposite of the sadist: he has a powerful and overwhelming superego, and nothing else. The sadist's superego is so strong that he has become identified with it; he is his own superego and can only find an ego in the external world. (124)

The masochistic fantasies of *Venus in Furs* are better understood as tableaux; there is not so much the literality of a subject-to-subject relation depicted, but a mis-en-scène in which each element is to be considered as both related and as strangely autonomous. Freud adopted the same "rhebus" method for reading the dream, when he reads the fantasy according to its textuality in the essay on *A Child Is Being Beaten.*

The fantasy that "a child is being beaten" is a common masochistic fantasy reported by women in analysis with Freud, and his examination of it neither pathologizes their desire—"Very probably there are still more frequent instances of it among the far greater number of people who have not been obliged to come to analysis by manifest illness" (Freud 1919, 179)—nor denies their pleasure in it. On the contrary, his analysis is spent accounting for the complicated "reality" to which the fantasy refers.

The fantasy is first reported as one from early school days, often aided by "morally masochistic" children's literature such as *Uncle Tom's Cabin:*

> The child began to compete with these works of fiction by producing his own phantasies and by constructing a wealth of situations and institutions, in which children were beaten, or were punished and disciplined in some way, because of their naughtiness and bad behaviour. (Freud 1919, 180)

The fantasy concludes with "an act of pleasurable auto-erotic satisfaction," although witnessing actual corporal punishment at school did not bring the same pleasure to the fantasists.

Analysis brings to light that "[t]he little girl's beating phantasy passes through three phases, of which the first and third are consciously remembered, the middle one remaining unconscious" (196). The first phase is built on sibling rivalry—beatings are desired for a sibling or other child, to prove that this child is not as loved as she; the textual motif is *"my father is beating the child whom I hate."* It is the second, unconscious, phase, in which the child herself is beaten by her father, which carries with it "the libidinal charge and the sense of guilt": *"I am being beaten by my father."*

In the third phase—the tableaux remembered from schooldays—the fantasy has changed again so that "it is almost invariably only boys who are being beaten. The person who does the beating is from the first her father, replaced later on by a substitute taken from the class of fathers." *A child is being beaten (on its naked bottom)* (ibid.).

Freud therefore has the girl-child rereading the earlier pleasure in the fantasy of "a child is being beaten" by force of the Oedipus complex—the desire for the father, and the subsequent penis envy. But the gendered character of this fantasy leads to the question under discussion only through a more general observation; that the fantasy is revised through the vicissitudes of the drive—in the feminine case reversals of aim and object which bring about femininity only imperfectly. Thus, the bodily pleasure of the masochistic tableau reflects a layering of erotic narrative, a sequence of imagined moments that form what one can justly call a "history of ideas."

This layering of bodily pleasure in erotic narrative is characteristic of fantasy in general and in fact explains the inception of sexuality, which is less a biological given than an intellectual construct, on this view. Laplanche and Pontalis, in their essay on *Fantasy and the Origins of Sexuality*, make this point: "The origin of fantasy cannot be isolated from the origin of the drive itself . . . sexuality is detached from any natural object and is handed over to fantasy, and, by this very fact, starts existing as sexuality" (Burgin 1986, 27–28).

The emergence of desire from the satisfaction of bodily need to which it originally attached *is* the formation of fantasy, that is, it is the inauguration of the feeling of satisfaction to be found in the image itself. Through this pathway, Freud imagines the generation of thought as such, thought as a detour taken by bodily affect through an itinerary of signs. Ironically, sex is usually imagined theoretically as the opposite of thought, and Freud's articulation of the mind in the service of the body is remarkable in light of it—I have described this process in greater detail in chapter 2 of *Passion in Theory*.

Thereafter, sexual pleasure is evidence of *thought* as much as of discharge, of mental as well as bodily processes. Autoerotic pleasure functions in this account as an important indicator of the change—the Freudian concept of the *experience of satisfaction* is reinterpreted, not as a stage of evolution of the drive, but instead as the moment that repeats the *disjunction* of sexual desire and bodily function. Masochism is thereby the exemplary case of sexuality, calling up the problem of the ontology of thought in an embodied and mortal creature. The layers of the "child is being beaten" fantasy illustrate the Freudian conception of a passage of the drive toward satisfaction through the field of mental representations, postulating a desire for which satisfaction can only come in the form of an image or idea.

The "dehiscence," or splitting, in intrapsychical relations, depicted as such a feature of the perversions of masochism and sadism, is analyzed by Lacan as a general property of self-consciousness. Ambivalence in the individual, in which an internal relation to oneself is experienced as so intensely contradictory that it must be lived outside the body in the figure of someone else, breaks apart completely only in pathological states, but emerges as the ontological tendency of subjectivity itself.

In Lacan's reading of Freud, language is the expedient that retrieves the subject from the extremes of Severin's fate; this "turning inside out." By instituting the possibility of the substitution of words for things, it brings the apparatus of definition to bear; and a separation can be instituted that is symbolized rather than literalized.

But in each subject, the crisis of this splitting is lived as a function of language in the most general sense. For Lacan, experience is the bodily pulse of the drive known in its itinerary through a world of signs.

This creates the possibility that is "transference"; the drive moves through the virtual space of psychical representations, and these representations are "pieces" of an outside world, the love-objects and objects of knowledge held by the subject in his mirror-gaze. They are, in effect, "signifiers," affixed for moments of being to states of internal demand, and they necessarily stand for them as their approximation. They remain provisional, for the same reason that, in Freud, the image could not represent that aspect of the instinct which is purely energy or force. For Lacan, the relation of mind-image to body-force, is an ontological relation: "Being" is the potential of the drives and their mental adoptives, taken together (the structure of "psychical reality," as described by Laplanche and Pontalis).

This suggests a rapport between the psychical and the social, at the inception of thought, in the very formation of concepts. For example, in the copula, which might be thought of as a structuring of psychical reality, the intellectual procedure of the "definition" appears isomorphic with the psychical operation called "repression"—an important and underemphasized consequence of Lacanian psychoanalysis. It would locate the "going between" of psychological and social theory as occurring in the context of thought as a kind of sign. And it rejoins Deleuze's concern with a critical, rather than a clinical, reading of the masochist's symptom.

Without this "aesthetic" inflexion, it is probable that psychoanalysis cannot meet the demands of feminism. An interpretation of the "between" of the psychical and the social, that presents a disembodied yet individualized psyche in a preexisting social reality, begs the question of the constitution of one in the other as an event. This can only result in a gender *in*difference, because it cannot take into analysis the gender difference as a difference arising through the body. On the other hand, an account that rests on an "aesthetic" underpinning can prove vital to the feminist analysis. This sensibility allows an understanding of the relation of materiality to signification that does not oppose them. The body would be depicted, on this sensibility, as flesh in the process of being subjected to a symbolic order, and in this subjection, yielding visceral sensations as concepts specific to that body and experienced as thought. This ontology, I would further argue and to rejoin the discussion in the first chapters of this book, gestures toward the mechanism by which the maternal body, too, might have its own ideas of things.

This can return us to the paradox with which I began this chapter. Through the prism of such a sensibility, one might glimpse the masochist as a subject whose pleasure is also her pain. And in doing so, catch an even more fleeting glimpse of the desire that lies behind her *thoughts*, her political ideas no less than her sexual fantasies being products of the structure of this embodied imaging.

A GENEROUS READING OF THE BODY

Other bodies in close proximity to one another can experience the phenomenology of merging with another as contentment; for example, the woman in love, and the pregnant woman.

Rosalyn Diprose and Iris Marion Young apply the phenomenology of Merleau-Ponty's work, in which it is the body and not the mind that is the site of subjectivity, to the case of feminine embodiment. A theorist for whom the aesthetic sensibility discussed above is central, Merleau-Ponty develops a philosophy of the body that allows for the way in which subjects may not find it easy to change, despite an intellectual awareness of questions of violence and oppression, as well as suggesting a pathway for change unlike more conventional "consciousness raising" through the modifying of bodily habits.

In *Throwing like a Girl*, Iris Marion Young takes the phenomenological paradigm explicitly into feminist theory, using, as she attests, a humanist feminist perspective that "superimposes Simone de Beauvoir's framework for describing women's existence in male-dominated society on Merleau-Ponty's framework for describing the lived body" (Wetton 1998, 287).

> Beauvoir describes women's situation in male-dominated society as that of being forced to live out a contradiction. Masculine culture and male desire position her as the Other, an objectified projection of masculine dreams and fears. Much about her life is in this way confined to making herself into an object. . . . Within this Beauvoirian framework, the strategy "Throwing like a girl" follows is to articulate a set of contradictory modalities of feminine body comportment, motility and spatiality. (287)

But twenty years on, Young points to the changes of embodiment for women, indicating "pathways for change"; the possibility of allowing girls to wear trousers, rather than skirts; the deemphasizing for women of the imperative on them to be "prim and proper"; interventions on the body such as contraception, allowing different expressions of the feminine body. Yet she has been surprised at the continuing currency of her analysis.

The omission of the difference of gendered bodies is a curious myopia in Merleau-Ponty's work, otherwise so sensitive to the morphologies that locate the particular body in its environment. (This omission is there in Foucault, as well, and one would almost detect an active *dis*interest in that possibility, in theorists otherwise so insightful.) Nevertheless, and despite Merleau-Ponty's grappling with a universal aspiration, which is perhaps a product of his scientific desires, his work lends itself to the differentiation of embodied beings, as Iris Marion Young suggests.

Simone de Beauvoir too attempts to modify a general description offered by the existential humanism of Sartre to the case of women, and finds in the process that gender limits the expression of humanity for one-half of it. For example, "throwing like a girl" attracts general derision and is a motif for the subject who cannot use her whole body in the action; the body is not viewed as an extension of that subjectivity, so much as the site of its contradiction.

Young wonders whether twenty years of feminist influence might not have had its own effects on the phenomenology of feminine motility, adjusting the modalities of bodily inhabitation and the contradictions between being subject/object and transcendence/immanence. But as it happens feminism has not yet transformed the relation between men and women in which women are objectified.

Young asks whether "being in one's body" needs to be thought on the instrumental view of the body, which is a masculine norm. What of the style of activity inherent in wearing high heels like weapons; the style of movement of a body through space which carries the baby on the hip—these point up other possibilities for the body's comportment, and "a description of women's body comportment and motility might also look for specifically valuable aspects of women's experience."

While apparently today a woman can choose between flat heels and high, she still does not get a choice about being an object at all. It is not necessarily a free choice, even if it is pleasurable to make choices that fashion oneself as an object of one's own choice. Being a subject-as-object is the feminine differentiation, as Young points out, for the masculine does not construct itself as an object in this way; it is not the masculine body's pleasure.

It can make a woman "feel better" to have her breasts made larger or smaller. But "cosmetic surgery" understates the way in which body modification can alter one's sense of oneself. Interestingly, Young is not claiming the masculine body is a more comfortable body to live. But she points to the different construction of subjectivity as it happens through the body—the feminine body being objectified differently from the masculine marks a difference between masculine and feminine subjectivity.

Whereas women get an ambivalent pleasure from being recognized as an object, masculine subjectivity is traditionally not satisfied with being interpreted as object. Is today the concern with commodity and desire producing masculine subjectivity more along the lines of the feminine? Has it reduced sexual difference in a direction opposite to that proposed by "feminism of equality"? The anxiety about "effeminacy" is expressed in ways as different as concerns about estragen in the environment, and Christopher Lasch's "culture of narcissism." But these anxieties overlook that it is as much a problem for the masculine as for the feminine that the subject of the copula is incoherent.

The feminist critique of phenomenology is one Young is keen to raise in relation to her earlier work—the distinction between transcendence and immanence, she notes, has been rightly criticized as incoherent by deconstructive feminists such as Butler. And Diprose raises a wider concern in respect to the dichotomies that are thought to govern bodies, asking whether "it would be wrong to generalize about the relation between gender identity and comportment as such restrictions would vary with differences in race and class." She suggests that the "synchronic relation to the other" maintained in Merleau-Ponty's view of the body would allow that "women's body comportments would be more multifarious and open to change than Young's analysis implies" (Diprose 2002, 202n).

To love and to desire are to open oneself to the body of the other in a way that makes explicit the mechanism by which the subject is inherently given its subjectivity through the other. Thus, loving and desiring are only extreme cases of a "generosity" that underwrites the whole possibility of subjectivity, on Diprose's account, and which makes each of us in relation to the other.

> I cannot exist otherwise than by risking my body integrity in an ambiguous situation, and freedom is nothing more or less than this. . . . The pleasure and pain of both love and the sexual encounter lie in the way that this risk becomes explicit. (90)

Using this account to engage the feminist anxiety about "safe sex," sado-masochism, and pornography, Diprose concludes, "Sex is never safe if safety means securing one's body integrity" (92). But this does not mean that there is no such thing as abuse. On the contrary, there is a "parsimony" that, in disregarding one's own bodily comportment, violates one's being:

> [F]or Merleau-Ponty, the corporeal self is constituted in relation to others who are already social beings . . . and the kind of body conducts we develop undergo a process of "sedimentation." Hence each of us develops a habitual way of patterning existence, including its erotic dimension, and the character of this patterning depends on the social and institutional setting in which our embodiment, and hence our world, is constituted.

Sexual difference is a bodily difference and this will be reflected in differences in body comportment and sexuality. "Alterity is maintained in the synchronic relation to the other," and "women's erotic styles will be multifarious despite any apparent patterns in comportment along the lines of sexual difference" (91–92).

> Granting limits to erotic generosity in this way effectively extends the concepts of violation and nonconsent beyond domination and submission in sex and particularizes the same concepts in terms of the specificity of a person's social, intercorporeal history. This is a necessary move, and not just because "domination" and "submission" can be consensual and hence without violation. Conversely, it also helps account for why a person can feel violated to the core of his or her being (through verbal abuse or physical intimidation, for example) in situations where to others he or she may appear open to anything at all and hence in situations that an outside observer may not consider sexual or serious. (93)

Perhaps the physical reorientation of the relation between self and world is terrifying to those philosophers accustomed to control through intellect, and to living the detached and docile body demanded and produced by that. The philosopher's body is a paradigm of it. But the philosopher's body is not the only body in existence, despite its privilege to speak conceptually of itself.

> [T]he philosopher describes sensations and their substratum as one might describe the fauna of a distant land—without being aware that he himself perceives, that he is the perceiving subject and that perception as he lives it belies everything that he says of perception in general. (1962, 207)

For Merleau-Ponty, the intellectual interpretations made on the world of objects including one's own body, is preceded by a layer of experience to which it gives rise, and to which one can have access only if one is prepared to suspend cultural and intellectual being long enough to contemplate how it is formed.

> For, seen from the inside, perception owes nothing to what we know in other ways about the world, about *stimuli* as physics describes them and about the sense organs as described by biology. It does not present itself in the first place as an event in the world to which the category of causality, for example, can be applied, but as a re-creation or re-constitution of the world at every moment. (207)

A kind of conceptuality that is the habit of a kind of body can be linked with Freud's anatomy of thought and its bodily origin. The thought that originates in the body, originates differently for different bodily comportments. The multifarious thought of bodies makes room even for the cyborg thought proposed by Haraway, but for which a rationalist science denies an ontological place.

The philosopher's body is a specific body, for which sublimation is the significant figure. The gender of this figure is implicated in the alignment of mind and body with the masculine/feminine distinction. But the apparatus of sublimation is constructed to distil clear ideas in their distinction out of the ambivalent flux of affective experience. Hard though it may be for this body to conceive of a conceptuality that is not clear and distinct, nevertheless it is only one body among many others, perhaps unimaginable in their being. These bodies have their own ideas, born of experience, and they have a syntax also for their thought. Exotic bodies suggest themselves as examples—the body that accepts scarification, the body that performs hard labor—but it might be more telling to draw on the ubiquitous bodies in the philosophical body's vicinity; the maternal and the erotic.

To the extent that philosophy is governed by this requisite bodily relation to the world, as separated from sensation, which is subordinated and distanced, then philosophy as a specific conception of being, is sheltered from other conceptions of being. Conversely, feminism has shown, there are missing from philosophy the concepts for the being of the maternal body, and the being of the erotic body.

If concepts render experience legible, the fact that the maternal or the erotic in philosophy is rendered as predicate and not subject, is not just an exclusion for feminism but a shortcoming for philosophy. It means that philosophy's concepts leave out what is needed to approach philosophically the phenomenon of sexual oppression. The concept of affect (in its pain) and of subjectivity (in the experience of it) brings the feminist to philosophy with resources that are missing in philosophy, and which it needs.

Perhaps the particular bodily posture that philosophy is, and the desire that it harbors, is not able to supervise the conceptuality needed for the invention of a philosophy of bodily oppression. Since it is her identity that is given in this experience, the feminist philosopher might need to go beyond the reasonable to find an analysis of it. Through her contact with love and violence she might work out how to do philosophy; through the erotic, and maternal where she experiences this undoing of identity, she also experiences the making of it, thereby understanding as a matter of physical gravity the importance of definition. Such a metaphysics could not be slandered as the abstruse, cerebral folly of intellect; it might be understood as a diagnostics of pain, subordination, and self-formation. Sensibility, the feminine, erotics, and maternity become a necessary preface to philosophy.

NINE

The Technology of Genre

No one lives in this room
without confronting the whiteness of the wall
behind the poems, planks of books,
photographs of dead heroines.
Without contemplating last and late
The true nature of poetry. The drive
To connect. The dream of a common language.
. . .
No one sleeps in this room without
The dream of a common language

—Adrienne Rich, *Origins and History of Consciousness*

Like it or not, I was born kin to Pu^{239} *and to transgenic, transspecific, and transported creatures of all kinds; that is the family for which and to whom my people are accountable.*

—Donna Haraway, *Modest_Wtiness@Second_Millenium*

The "assisted reproductive technologies," although publicized under a clinical fascia as treatment for the medical condition of infertility, now leach into the more speculative realms of genetic manipulation, providing the techniques for cloning, foetal tissue research, and germ line patenting. As feminist writers on biotechnology have noted, this modification of "life" proceeds apace, and under the aegis of capitalist production, commodification, and accumulation.

Radical adventures in technoscience threaten us with new life forms, which Donna Haraway, in the above quote, embraces as kin. Technology produces change, sometimes dramatic change, in the material world. Its innovation can be seen to exceed the thought that engendered it. This is not only a property of technology but of any reproduction. In reproduction, something is produced of a kind that was there before and yet that is also new; reproduction must produce that which is "the same, only different" (to quote a colloquial definition of genre cf. Lacy 2000). The innovation in technology is genuinely reproductive and by my argument, generic, since it *produces new matter of the same kind.*

But how can such innovation be possible, let alone ubiquitious as today it threatens to become? It has been a stalwart theoretical prejudice, that there is a distinction to be observed between the representation and the reality of things. Feminist theory has suffered from this distinction as much as any, and more generally, has suffered from distinction *as such*—one could say its warrant comes from the distinction between the sexes. This chapter explores the challenge that reproductive technology, in its generic action, presents.

Teresa de Lauretis proposed, in 1987, that feminist theorists follow Foucault, and pose a technology of gender that would discover its productive field in "the set of effects produced in bodies, behaviours and social relations" by the deployment of "a complex political technology" (1987, 3). Acknowledging that Foucault's own work on a technology of sex "excludes, though it does not preclude, the consideration of gender," de Lauretis anticipated in her line of argument an approach that Judith Butler has become differently—and more famously—known for. Butler's theoretical amalgam of European and American political philosophy specifically understands gender as performative, allied to strands of thought in Nietzschean and pragmatist philosophy, while de Lauretis's deployment of the concept of discursive technology is perhaps more specifically psychoanalytic, Foucauldian, and structuralist. Nevertheless, similar intuitions are expressed in the notion of a technology of gender productive of lived representations, and a performativity of gender understood through bodies, read as signs by other bodies.

"Gender is (a) representation," de Lauretis asserts, and "the representation of gender *is* its construction" (3). Thus, the political technology that produces gender continues its work today, despite the changes in the representations of gender engendered by second wave feminism;

and indeed this knowledge forces upon de Lauretis the conclusion that "the construction of gender is also effected by its deconstruction."

The technology of gender is a fabrication of material and of signs; "[T]he sex-gender system, in short, is both a sociocultural construct and a semiotic apparatus." While de Lauretis thereby makes a clear case for gender as a representation, she does not quite make of representation a material, despite the discussion of film as a technology of representations. This, perhaps, flows from de Lauretis following Althusser more closely than Foucault. The fissure bothered de Lauretis herself: she described it as the constant slippage between "Woman as representation" and "women as historical beings" that feminist theory is founded on.

It is through technology that its bifurcation is challenged. No longer is the proposition that "Woman is a representation" a preposterous postmodern slur; and in contemporary terms, the postulate of a historical being *outside* representation emerges as just as unconvincing. The separation of being from representation is compromised by the action of technology, as I shall argue. This action gives material to thought; technology, especially reproductive technology, is ontological in a highly virulent way. ARTs (the abbreviation commonly given to the assisted reproductive technologies) give material effect to representations. No sooner is the gene identified than it is able to become the subject of "genetic modification"—the thought of the code allowing a whole textual expression to be given to life, which now sequences itself according to a syntactical vision. As Sarah Franklin has observed, when the discourse shifts from gene to cell, more ecological properties are discerned, and then deployed, in the manipulation of conception (Franklin 2004, unpublished paper).

So does technology effortlessly enmesh matter in rhetoric, and subject in substance, subjecting it also to a commodifying homogeneity. The effects of this synthesis remain a challenge to feminist thinking.

FROM KIND TO BRAND

The theory that seeks to capture the value production inherent in representation needs to leave open the space of difference, or in the technical terms of deconstruction (whose work this is) *the spacing of différance.* And a grasp of the material nature of this production must let go of preexistent normativities, for it is only in surrendering the valencies already invested in signs that new values can be seen for themselves.

But to let go of valency is also to surrender political and ethical norms; perhaps nowhere more than in the work of Donna Haraway is this struggle between *difference* and *norm* in a feminist vision of technoscience more puzzling and more intense. On the side of difference, Haraway's theoretical directions converge in three conjunctive possibilities:

- *Irony*, or, the postulate that representations matter; to quote her, she has "an ironic dream of a common language for women in the integrated circuit"
- *The Cyborg*, or, technology as a viable mode of political life; "I'd rather be a cyborg than a goddess"
- *Perspective*, or situated knowledges; the best sense we can make of scientific objectivity is a "positioned rationality"

In bringing unthought possibilities to life, the means of expression is critical. Different theoretical and political aims call for different orderings, different genres. This may be why Haraway writes *manifesto;* for cyborgs, intended to galvanize and to act as a position statement for an "ironic dream of a common language for women in the integrated circuit"; for companion species, adjuring: "Run fast; bite hard!"

And, valorizing the action of the trope, Haraway writes: "I think of anti-racist feminist literacy as a process of learning to build a world of reference to and with those who engage freedom projects through the many-stranded lives of specifically located, historically diverse women." Adopting the metaphor of the reef, she cherishes an "[e]nlightenment sort of hope" that "[s]uch a feminist standpoint is . . . a circulating and salty fluid of bodies and meanings" (Olson and Hirsh 1995, xii).

In looking to varieties of representation beyond scientific fact and theoretical argument, Haraway focuses rhetorical energy on language and signification as agents of political change. She calls on figures such as irony and metaphor, and genres like manifesto and rhapsody, where questions of representation and expression affect the very objects of which they speak. By exploring and exploiting the different expressive powers within empirical language in particular, Haraway is more than describing a world, she is producing a set of possibilities in it *through writing*, by engaging different representational practices.

She writes of this activist representation, that it grows out of her own biography, having "learned to read and write inside worlds at war":

> These worlds at war are the belly of the monster from which I have tried to write into a more vivid reality a kin group of

feminist figures. My hope is that these marked figures might guide us to a more livable place, one that in the spirit of science fiction I have called "elsewhere." (Haraway 2004, 2)

And while declaring "I am in love with biology," she has "a perverse love of words," employing figures and tropes, because they are "a way of swerving around a death-defying and death-worshipping culture bent on total war, in order to re-member—in material-semiotic reality—the fragile, mortal, and juicy beings we really are" (2).

Modest_Witness@Second_Millenium (Haraway 1997) is so layered with the examples and fragments of this project that it groans under the weight—perhaps creating the very value-disintegration that Haraway fears, or at least mimicking a relativist chaos that elsewhere in her philosophy of science she has been at pains to subdue. But a manifesto lays down the law—the cyborg manifesto is more focused, if more didactic.

The position is evoked as an "ironic dream," irony being a trope that produces its meaning through a doubling. Haraway's epistemology holds the hope of knowledge, but not knowledge produced as univocal truth. Rather, truth will resonate in a double meaning, produced ironically. Since irony produces its effect in a meaning that takes shape differently from that which it consciously expresses, Haraway can also express skepticism about the "fact" of these technological matters while acknowledging their material reality.

At the same time, a dream of a "common language" would seek expression for what women have in common, allowing them to find their interests in common in the "integrated circuit," a globalized network where, Haraway points out, their interests are at risk of being eclipsed. The products of the military-industrial complex, the history of the evolution of these technologies, funded from conservative funds and national interests in defense, communications, and population control and demographic sciences, do not have feminist aims in view. The manifesto demands that women take back for their kind some expertise in relation to the network spread over ordinary lives, or otherwise they may become less powerful the more caught up in it they become.

"We do not need a totality to work well. The feminist dream of a common language, like all dreams for a perfectly true language, of perfectly faithful naming of experience, is a totalizing and imperialist one." Will the dream of a strategic language, which lives only on expedient common ground fare better? Haraway describes a feminism that does not have a stable object, one which can find its political interests at the intersection of several shifting discourses. Given that it shifts, feminist thinkers will need to formulate continually different approaches, in order to articulate powerlessness in relation to gender position, wherever it is produced. But at no stage does this suggest that the normativity in feminist politics is inappropriate or superceded. Rather, its modes have shifted, its rationality reordered but its affects still hold. This, according to Haraway, makes it more important to find the strategic alliance between people of different discursive interests, and to set normativities in motion across unstable signifying landscapes.

For Haraway, theory itself becomes a political practice, as the manifesto genre shows; it is not effective for feminist theory to turn away from poststructuralism as if it were mere game playing in language, since the challenge to unified truth and stable meaning has long since come about. Haraway desires a style of truth production that is not empirically self-evident, but involved in social and historical forces in a knowing way. "This chapter is an effort to build an ironic political myth faithful to feminism, socialism and materialism," she writes.

Haraway's famous slogan from this early essay is: "I'd rather be a cyborg than a goddess." (cf. Lykke and Braidotti 1996). This admiration for technology is not shared by all feminists, and there are those who do not feel particularly safe with the cyborg, even if the goddess is today claustrophobic. But the choice may not be as stark as that between a bold cyborg and an old goddess—the vision is of "[a]n elsewhere born out of the hard (and sometimes joyful) work of getting on together in a kin group that includes cyborgs and goddesses working for earthly survival" (2004,3). Haraway dares us to reconceive the social world, including that between bodies, on the model of technology rather than in resistance to it.

It could be said that this has already started to happen. Through medical science, the body is produced as a technology. The drug has long since been reconceived from spiritual action—an altered state induced by a sacred substance—to a technological process that intervenes in the body, and into its processes, going to work on them. Technology associated with our concepts of work, as means-and-ends, is powerfully invested in the medical body. The thought of the "prosthetic" has its clear emblem in the penis as tool and as power, its castration as the fear of a loss of rationality and law. Assisted reproduction thus comes on the horizon not as a "new technology" but as the end point of a dominant style of thought. And Haraway's work, like other timely feminist writing, warns against misunderstanding what the technological world has made or is making of women's biology.

But, more positively than many feminist writers, Haraway hopes the thought of the cyborg might liberate us from oppositional logic. The "ironic political myth" of the cyborg aims to challenge borders and boundaries, calling into question oppositions that have founded Western epistemology and metaphysics; human/animal, organism/machine, physical/nonphysical.

The cyborg vision is purposefully upbeat: "I like to imagine . . . a cyborg society . . . committed to building a political form that actually manages to hold together witches, engineers, elders, perverts, Christians, mothers, and Leninists long enough to disarm the state." It engages a democracy, explicitly thought in terms of the "holding together" of a "common interest."

In a key paper on the possibility of feminist knowledge, Haraway writes:

> The science question on feminism is about objectivity as positioned rationality. Its images are not the products of escape and transcendence of limits (the view from above) but the joining of partial views and halting voices into a collective subject position that promises a vision of the means of ongoing finite embodiment, of living within limits and contradictions—of views from somewhere. (259)

This offers an account of knowledge that allows for valid assertions while also describing a necessarily partial perspective in all knowledge in virtue of its situation. Such a description would not discount that some knowledges might differ (and even conflict?) with other knowledges about women and their meanings.

Each of these three diverse postulates of Haraway's theorizing point to the significance of differences for the imagining of new theoretical and political possibility. *Irony* is operative through the difference between the statement and the referent. The *cyborg* allows life to differ, to depart from a preexistent nature. *Situated knowledges* install difference in rationality because they entail a perspectival conviction as to truth.

However, competing with these possibilities for difference in Haraway's work are norms, derived from an underlying liberal-democratic model of politics, which deflect their potential.

Conversation replaces discourse; "Accounts of a 'real' world do not, then, depend on a logic of 'discovery' but on a power-charged social relation of 'conversation,'" Haraway writes in the influential paper on situated knowledges. The production of knowledge is redirected from an intelligibility that emerges from power as its discourse, toward the very different democratic virtue of conversation. While this view is presented in the context of a challenge to scientific objectivity, it does not grasp the nettle of the Foucauldian critique of it (of, for example,

Les Mots et Les Choses). More to the point, in proposing knowledge to come out of the "social relation" of conversation, the conditions for the possibility of communication are already assumed. Even as Haraway acknowledges that the relation can be "power-charged," the trope of conversation commits others to speaking a common language, or at least to consenting to translation, and so rendering unintelligible any radically different utterance.

"Situated knowledges require that the object of knowledge be pictured as an actor and agent . . ." (259). This actor would then be figured as a subject in the object position; but deconstruction suggests that mere reversal of these positions will not disarm the "power-charged" relations of which Haraway writes. While conversation is a fundamental tool of the democratic, is not the same thing as discourse. A conversation that is power charged is likely to be an unequal exchange, despite the value of equal representation that is being invoked. Discourse can be conceived of as power charged in a wholly other sense; the difference is seen in the contrast between the conversation that articulates a position, and the discourse that produces it.

Further, in the transformation of the object of knowledge into actor, agency replaces the plurality of the events. The uncanny challenge of the cyborg (and even the mystic power of a goddess) is subjected to the rational actor, whose world is always and already a stage on which he performs his agency. Nothing is fortuitous in this vision, nothing is given, or left, to chance.

Haraway's explicit rhetoric aims to mobilize tropes in the direction of producing a new political *myth*, one that could produce meaning for a feminist endeavor. Kinship and reproduction are already powerfully mythic, as writers such as Sarah Franklin (1997; 2001) have shown. But can one produce myth so consciously? In invoking myth to a didactic end, it is not clear that Haraway can animate the elemental layer in which such affective figures arise.

Haraway draws attention to the appropriating habits of capital, and reinvents kinship as a more communitarian virtue, the "kinship of feminist figurations." "I am riveted by 'brand names' and 'genders'; that is, as generic marks that are directional signals on maps of power and knowledge," she writes. "Property is the kind of relationality that poses as the-thing-in-itself, the commodity, the thing outside relationship" (8). If "kind" and "brand" are generic, then the brand name is the mark of equivalence, while gender is the mark of difference. An explicit commodifying of interest holds the list of the cyborg's "strategic allies" together, and in so doing, gives expression to the conceptual kinship of democracy with technology. Strategic alliance will give birth to common interests among limited others, for whom other alliances might represent competition. This democracy is a commodity politics, but flattening difference in this discursive commonality risks obscuring the production of value in other genres.

For example, only in a particular discursive coupling can the interest of the pervert find common expression with the Christian, or the witch with the engineer. In other discursive worlds, the "situation" of the Christian and the pervert are not on the same map. And, where is the Islamicist on this ground? Common interest among these others is reduced to an unspecific demand for political recognition. But a relativist rationality that assumes situations are equivalent for the point of view of their truth value, undermines the point of its perspectivalism, and risks producing all principle as a commodity equivalent to any other worldview "on the market."

Indeed, the "situated knowledges" that underpin democratic practice for Haraway express a radically obscure epistemology, in which the situation from which the knowledge is perceived is nevertheless potentially the equivalent of any other situation. This equivalence of position makes judgment possible, but at the expense of a radical difference that cannot be represented in the same discourse. This is revealed, I suggest, in the rhetorical shock value of the list Haraway provides of those who might disarm the State. Leninists, mothers, and Christians? Beyond their humanity, *what* common project, *what* political agency do they share? It is hard to see in what guise this commonality could be coherent, let alone welcome.

The contrary motion in Haraway's vision between difference and the norm results in a *situational equivalence* without significant distinguishing features. The theoretical action—which was also conceived as a political action—becomes becalmed in opposing tendencies that cancel one another out. This outcome is all the more puzzling for being quite contrary to the rhetoric, which is designed to galvanize.

ART BECOMES ART

To find the vector of such conflicts of perspective one would need to ask whether there is a perspective from which these situated knowledges might *interest each other*. For example, in what way does women's desire for independence become a brand of cigarettes ("You've come a long way, baby")?

Or, in what ways do the technologies of gender and the operations of capital conjoin to produce the fear-desire of the "designer baby," a phantom of the commodification of life? The contemporary bioethical community adjudicates on whether knowledge—the technique to make this paradigm of choice a reality—should even be uncovered and regulatory bodies decide whether to authorize foetal tissue research (cf. Franklin and McKinnon 2001 for absorbing discussions of capitalism and biotechnology).

If knowledge becomes a commodity like any other in the postmodern world, let us recall how the commodity comes to be a kind of fetishism.

> The metamorphosis of value is a tale about man, his productive activity and products, and what happens to them all in capitalist society. Misreading this story as one about the activities of inanimate objects, attributing to them qualities which only human beings could possess, positing living relations for what is dead, is what Marx calls the "fetishism of commodities." (Ollman 1971)

Commodification gives an object or thing meaning wholly within a universe constituted by desires. The commodity gratifies my purposes, has value inasmuch as it is fit for my ends. Of course, the uncanny aspect to the commodity—that it generates value *merely by differing from what it in fact is*—was noted by Marx. But here it also emerges that the commodity is essentially technological, when viewed in these terms; the commodity embodies a relation between subject and object, and as such, the commodity is the product of instrumental thinking.

And the commodity is a precondition of capital.

> It cannot be overemphasised that capital is based on exchange. "The circulation of commodities is the starting point of capital." (Capital I 146) Marx saw the historical development of the market system in terms of the erosion of the feudal mode of production by the extension of exchange which gradually transformed the purpose of production. (Roberts and Stephenson 1973, 37)

This suggests that by definition capital is committed to technology (this proposition has long underpinned the analyses of the Frankfurt School). Further, it sketches a kinship between democratic liberalism, capital, and technology from the perspective of *exchange value.* While the laudable value of political equality seems at odds with the normalizing of technological progress and the global reduction of capital, there is nevertheless a thread that binds these three terms in their mode of value-production: *equivalence promotes exchange.*

Democracy, too, is a kind of technology, a product of the rationality that orders the world according to the subject/object (means/ends) style of thought. As a political genre, democracy fits technology as a subject/object ordering and it also fits well with the commodity, which is a product of the same distinction. Technology produces an ethos of exchange, so that if there is a state of being that is not expressible within that instrumental rationality then its being is at risk; the cyborg here could become an oppressive vision.

The technological contains these aspects, feminism and consumerism, as "isms" in a generic discourse. That is, both desires are now exploited as generic vehicles for the carriage of social action, and generic brands for political consumption. The concept of a capitalist economy is built on exchange, and relies on a style of value-production that operates through norms. Feminist equals Marxist equals Anarchist but does not equal terrorist. The economy is a brilliant myth, for we cannot imagine living without it—an economic arrangement where no one is paid, and no one has rights is today incredible, or rather, desire for it is incredible, despite this having been the condition of women in many histories.

The citizen is like the dollar and follows similar laws. When democracy is the political currency, then money is the model and the tool of value (the tool being an indicator of technological thought). It remains a metaphysical assumption that a society is a system for the exchange of rights among equal units of citizenry.

Haraway calls her theoretical vision "myth" as a generative principle of meaning. Myth is that which cannot be disproven, since it is the foundation of "justified belief" in a particular social world. Like the economy, technology is a myth of this order, for to deny it makes no sense. To describe the world with other than technological truth protocols can result in incomprehensibility. For example, to say "the world was created in seven days" is to be just "wrong"—we "know" the world was created through the Big Bang or a similar scientific postulate, such an idea functioning for most of us as an article of faith.

To take another example, "the world is flat"; when one looks out of the window, one might reflect that this is not a "silly" idea so much as a superceded myth. The world *is* flat to a phenomenological purpose that moves across it—when does the pedestrian experience the curvature of the globe? But the discourse that describes the world as round is a myth of a different order, one which is functional and comprehensible within the technological order and which is completely relied on today, such that we are all convinced of it without most of us having had any "firsthand" experience of it. To deny it is "heresy" and leads to discursive ostracism. We cannot use the idea of a flat world.

It is worth asking for what end do we use the idea of a *round* world? Globalization is probably the most dramatic application of it—the coherence of the round form of the world gives substance to this imaginary process that is now very real. The test of any myth is not whether it is unthinkable that it should be wrong, but whether, without it, one can *inhabit* that particular generic world at all.

The generic world that includes feminism might also be mythical at least in this sense: that it would be accurate to depict feminist knowledge as an epistemic claim generated by the effects of the subject of modernity and, in particular, from its collaboration with capitalism. We have already seen that both are conceptually generated from technology, that is, from instrumental rationality. And so it follows from this that feminism, too, is a technology of gender (echoing de Lauretis).

Foucault is one of a handful of philosophers for whom technology emerges as an ontological reagent, appearing in an order of discursive materiality. The paradox arising in the concept of technology is most eloquently put by Heidegger: "[T]he origin of technology is nothing technological." Technology, while being the most material of events—indeed, it is definitive of materialism—is first and foremost a way of thinking, a way of representing the material world. "Technology is therefore no mere means. Technology is a way of revealing," as he writes (Heidegger, 318). In the *Essay concerning Technology*, this way of thinking about technology takes us beyond its material surfaces to a unique conceptual configuration—a style of rationality constructed out of the instrumental character of means and ends, out of human purpose and agency.

This conception of rationality in turn is grounded in a distinction between subject and object that isolates one in the terms of the other. The subject/object distinction appears as a grammatical function, produced through the copula, which is the means of distinction in general. But the subject/object distinction also has its resonance in understanding the social domain—subjectivity, and its relation to language, having been shown in twentieth century philosophy to be determinative. Heidegger himself constructs a version of this conviction in the notion of the poetic, but the assumption is also influential in the work of (post)structuralists such as Lacan, Foucault, and of the "Frankfurt School."

Because this conception of technology brings it to analysis as first and foremost a way of revealing, it opens a way for thinking technology that enlightens not only the aggressive innovations it has made in the material world, but also the conceptual innovation of an aesthetics that brings about the truths it conceives. Heidegger finds a common element in art and technology in his definition of "techne":

> *Technikon* means that which belongs to *techne*... *techne* is the name not only for the activities and skills of the craftsman but also for the arts of the mind and the fine arts. *Techne* belongs to bringing-forth, to *poiesis*; it is something poetic. (318)

So, in *The Origin of the Work of Art* Heidegger writes: "A building, a Greek temple, portrays nothing. . . . The building encloses the figure of the god. . . . By means of the temple, the God is present in the temple" (Heidegger 1977, 167). The ruined temple—far more than the van Gogh shoes, which have received so much more commentary from this essay—stand out in Heidegger's imagining of the aesthetic. It is architecture, sculpture, performance, and installation art—as the forming of space—that show us the prototype for the technological.

The concept of the aesthetic as a kind of forming suggests that the artistic product is not in principle different from any (other) technological innovation. The realism of the building or sculpture—even the painting—operates according to the same principles of realization; the production of an object that has as one of its aspects its "thingliness." And the "downstream" consequences of the production of these "things" are similarly complex in art and technology, the objects entering a cultural imaginary as well as finding a physical space for themselves; generating their habitat by inhabiting it.

This applies too to the technologies of reproduction, employed as realism, that create without irony and without intended self-reference. Creating the habitat for the IVF baby has been partly a matter of adding this real thing to a life-world. A twenty-first birthday party for the first baby created through IVF attracts even more congratulation than for the average young adult, and through it, Louise Brown proves simultaneously how ordinary and how extraordinary is her participation in life. Dolly, the celebrated sheep-clone, has two lambs the ordinary way and reproductive technology takes the world by stealth, since animal husbandry has always produced particular biological realities at the expense of others.

However, Heidegger's notion of thingliness calls for a distinction between art and equipment. The majority of technology manages to pass for equipment, since it is transparently a means for a solid end. The machine that digs holes creates a tunnel. But equipment is not distinct from art, it merely displays more naiveté as to the aesthetic properties of its composition. This production might be, not so much distinguished from "art," but likened to *bad* art, not in control of its extremities. Yet, there is a sensibility in art and technology that doesn't need consciousness of itself in order to exhibit its genius. Consider the "net-fridge," one in an array of "smart technologies" designed to reorganize the patterns of domestic consumption.

A refrigerator that replaces its own contents may seem to be an appliance with a small (and superfluous) talent. However, as an exercise in the connection of technology to commodity, it is instructive, since no sooner does it come on the market and the consumer become aware of its capacity, than the consumer also become aware, perversely, of the need for such a technology—its "convenience" and "common sense" leading one predictably toward *wanting* one. This *desire* is the presumption that technology shows in the face of the future. It means to change us, into the kind of life form that eats what the refrigerator decrees will be uploaded from the Internet supermarket.

The *oblivion* of the really good invention, the really new technology, is the hallmark of its equipmentality—technology is working when we don't notice it, when desire for it "seems natural" and "makes sense" (everyone needs a TV or mobile phone, everyone wants children), and when we take it for granted. At the same time, this oblivion is indicative of instrumental rationality, which obliterates the plausibility of any other thinking than functional thinking. "[T]he challenging-enframing not only conceals a former way of revealing, bringing-forth, but it conceals revealing itself and with it that wherein unconcealment, i.e. truth, comes to pass" (Heidegger 1977, 309). This is Heidegger's famous "danger of technology," an inherent tendency in the dominant rationality to proliferate its own thinking, and in the same operation rendering other styles of thought implausible.

But in the case of the ARTs, is the constraint of means/ends equipmentality any longer possible? When it is new life that is produced, might it not open up instead the revealing space of *alethea* which Heidegger gives to the thing known as art? The revealing of technology is a kind of truth-making, it is arguably a kind of "setting-to-work of truth." Does ART *become art*; its concern with organic reproduction taking on an uncanny aesthetic hue? Ironically, this is what some most feared from *postmodernism*, that it would *aestheticize life*, but in hindsight it seems they were merely blaming the messenger.

> Because the essence of technology is nothing technological, essential reflection upon technology and decisive confrontation with it must happen in a realm that is, on the one hand, akin to the essence of technology and, on the other, fun-

> damentally different from it. Such a realm is art. But certainly only if reflection upon art for its part, does not shut its eyes to the constellation of truth concerning which we are *questioning.* (Heidegger 1977, 317)

REPRODUCTION, SERIALITY, GENRE

The conventional positing of an ethics over against an aesthetics, a science versus an art, raises critical questions about the style of rationality engendering technological life. In what way can the distinction of a normative realm from a "purely" factual one be understood, in a world where the products of facts—technological devices and procedures—are producing their own "value-adding," new materialities that change the plausible commitments to categories as old as "life"?

Can we rely on the distinction of subject and object to distinguish a subjectivity from an objectivity, in a world where technological excesses are at least as proliferant as technological purposes? And I mean not only through the brave new worlds of biotechnology, but also in the global change brought on as environmental damage, global warming, species depletion, etc.? These are issues toward which a feminist discussion of technoscience can be addressed.

The logic of paradox is an important contributor to the strangeness engendered by the reproductive technologies. When understood as a grammatical structure, the distinction between subject and object gives us the attribution of identity per se: "I am that." And when analyzed as a logical relation, the difference between subject and object turns out to produce distinction *as such.* The copula is kin to technology. These concepts harbor a structural relation not immediately obvious on the surface; they are *ontologically active.* Technology, as the rationality of means and ends, is the thinking of subject and object; *technology is copulative* and by this very fact is reproductive. It "proliferates," it generates more of itself, it spawns whole series and installs itself as the thought of the real, the real as a proliferant seriality related by association. "I am that"; "I am not this."

To the extent that ethical and political arguments concerning reproductive technology accept the distinction between materiality and representation, they do not approach the issue as an ontological one. Their depictions of the future that the technology offers are unconvincing. Understanding feminism as itself a technology, that is, as a kind of thought whose conceptions—equality for women, for example—have become material events, throws new light on the reproductive technologies.

It raises the possibility that the theory that utilizes the discourses of the social sciences, no less than the life sciences, might bring its objects of analysis to life.

Technology challenges, but perhaps in a more subtle way than manifesto envisages. Its effects are due to an *exceeding* of its logic, of its copulative terms, rather than a liberation from them. Its challenge comes from a characteristic of representation Derrida described as *iterability*; a reproduction that is more than a repetition. It is an uncanny principle, indebted to seriality itself, that a sign must be repeatable, but is thereby "never the same *twice*." In assisting this reproduction, the category of "genre," as generative and as generic, could be called to play a part.

Genre is the concept of the *reproduction of order*; as literary genre governs the reproduction of texts, a sexuate genre with an inflection of a feminist kind could be understood to govern the reproduction of (social) life. In "genre theory," which not by accident grows up in the study of media and film, genre is that paradoxical principle that accounts for reproduction; the making of new text that is "the same, but different." Genre as the motor of reproduction must bring forth the new but in the context of the old, or risk the monstrous; a future recognizable to the past and continuous with the present, while novel enough not to seem to be mere repetition, as a "clone."

It is not surprising that the question of genre is most pressing in the areas of film and media, since these are areas most intimately sensitive to commercial success, and so to the commodification of the new. The commodity is a style of engenre-ing, and presents paradox in the world of things, as the literary genre presents to the text; its fetishistic tendency to make itself where it is not. The commodity, the reproduction, and the work of art now have a tangled engenrement, which was recognized as least as long ago as Walter Benjamin's essay 'The Work of Art in the Age of Mechanical Reproduction.' Benjamin asks whether the aura of the original can be saved from the ubiquitous reproduction of the printing press and the camera.

How much more will this be said of the era of the digital reproduction, in which the copy now reproduces itself and spreads as a "virus." But the ubiquity of digital reproduction not only fails to affirm the aura of the unique existent or art work; it undermines the status of the original and its claim to the aura of origin, even as it repeats it. Seriality introduces its own uncanny uniqueness, as John Frow (1998) argues; the uniqueness of the commodity as artwork becomes desired for its place in a series of signatures (for example, the series of things called "Warhol"). The author or artist becomes by this logic a commodity itself; eventually one cannot "tell the difference" between a seriality engendered by the reproduction or print from the absolute singularity of the commodified work of art, since the value of both is given fetishistically.

The involvement of media and film as itself a *field of technological evolution* draws attention to the generic processes of change and transformation. The communication of change happens through a series, or genealogy, rather than by narrative or argument, and emerges via elements constituted out of a recombinant code. It does so graphically, that is, according to the logic of the image, which it supports. Film begets television begets video begets DVD and the webcam . . . in this way, genre becomes genetic. This evolution puts to work the insight of structuralism; the binary heart of the code, distinguishable only in its difference, can nevertheless support assemblies of dizzying variety, whose principle of generation is generic—nothing other than "the same, but different."

Are we able to move beyond the binary, which is to say, to critique the technological? The pressure to do so surfaces in the very digital that is constituted in binarism, because through its iterability, the form proliferated by genre exceeds itself materially in every way. That is to say, that a generic world in which new life takes form will be called upon to reckon with whatever mode of being has been introduced, however normal, equivalent, or aspiring to the "selfsame." The superceding of sexual reproduction, if this is what is occurring in the reproductive technologies, is a *regenre-ing*, open to a heterogenous future.

"The principal characteristic of being responsible is this starting something on its way into arrival," Heidegger writes, of the "cause" of anything (1977, 292). The conception of a technology of genre would take responsibility for a production that was not its own, literally incorporating the paradox of change, and would engage with this risk and even relish it. A technology of genre is a conceptual technology that might start our reproduction, not on its way into the "selfsame," but into its arrival, whatever that may be. A copulative logic could reveal how instrumental rationality is haunted not merely by technological excesses but, more profoundly, by the marginal ontologies it engenders—the not-quite, the not-yet, and the maybe-never-to-be possibilities.

It might also engender feminist myths of technoscience, as Haraway hopes, and even support a correlative myth of feminism *as* technoscience, working toward the insight that technology presents both danger and the terms of its "saving power."

Bibliography

Adams, Alice. 1994. *Reproducing the womb: Images of childbirth in science, feminist theory, and literature.* Ithaca: Cornell University Press.

Albury, Rebecca. 1999. *The politics of reproduction: Beyond the slogans.* Sydney: Allen and Unwin.

Allen, Judith, and Paul Patton, eds. 1983. *Beyond Marxism? Interventions after Marx.* NSW: Intervention Publications.

Aries and Beijin. 1985. *Western sexuality: Practice and precept in past and present time.* Trans. Anthony Forster. Oxford: Blackwell.

Bair, Deirdre. 1990. *Simone de Beauvoir: A biography.* London : Jonathan Cape.

Barthes, Roland. 1982, c. 1977. "The metaphor of the eye." In Georges Bataille (Lord Auch), *Story of the Eye,* trans. Joachim Neugroschel, with essays by Susan Sontag and Roland Barthes. Harmondsworth: Penguin.

———. 1986. *The Rustle of Language.* Trans. Richard Howard. Oxford: Blackwell.

Bataille, Georges (Lord Auch). 1982, c.1977. *Story of the eye.* Trans. Joachim Neugroschel, with essays by Susan Sontag and Roland Barthes. Harmondsworth: Penguin.

———. 1962. *Eroticism: Death and sexuality.* Trans. Mary Dalworthy. San Francisco: City Lights.

Beauvoir, Simone de. 1963. *Memoirs of a dutiful daughter.* Harmondsworth: Penguin.

———. 1977. *The second sex.* Trans. and ed. H. M. Parshley. Harmondsworth: Penguin. (trans. of *Le Deuxieme sexe.* Paris: Gallimard, 1949)

Benjamin, Jessica. 1988. *The bonds of love: Psychoanalysis, feminism, and the problem of domination.* New York: Pantheon.

———. 1995. *Like subjects, love objects: Essays on recognition and sexual difference.* New Haven: Yale University Press.

Benjamin, Walter. 1936 (1969 ed.). "The work of art in the age of mechanical reproduction." In *Illuminations,* ed. Hannah Arendt, trans. Harry Zohn. New York: Schocken Books.

Benveniste, Emile. 1971. "The linguistic functions of to be and to have." In *Problems in general linguistics,* trans. Mary E. Meek. Coral Gables: University of Miami Press.

Bland, Lucy. 1995. *Banishing the beast: English feminism and sexual morality 1885–1914.* Harmondsworth: Penguin.

Bourke, C., N. Schor, and M. Whitford, eds. 1994. *Engaging with Irigaray.* New York: Columbia University Press.

Braidotti, Rosi. 1989. "The politics of ontological difference." In *Between feminism and psychoanalysis,* ed. Teresa Brennan. London and New York: Routledge.

Burgin, V., J. Donald, and C. Kaplan, eds. 1986. *Formations of fantasy.* London: Methuen.

Butler, Judith. 1990. *Gender trouble: Feminism and the subversion of identity.* New York: Routledge.

———. 1993. *Bodies that matter: On the discursive limits of sex.* New York: Routledge.

———. 1997. *The psychic life of power: Theories in subjection.* Stanford: Stanford University Press.

———, Ernesto Laclau, and Slavoj Zizek. 2000. *Contingency, hegemony, universality: Contemporary dialogues on the left.* London and New York: Verso.

Cannold, Leslie. 2005. *What, no baby? Why women are losing the freedom to mother, and how they can get it back.* North Fremantle: Curtin University Press.

Chanter, Tina. 1995. *Ethics of Eros: Irigaray's rewriting of the philosophers.* New York, London: Routledge.

———. 2001. *Time, death, and the feminine: Levinas with Heidegger.* Stanford: Stanford University Press.

Chodorow, Nancy. 1974. *Family structure and feminine personality.* Stanford: Stanford University Press (by the Trustees of the Leland Stanford Junior University).

Clarke, Adele. 1998. *Disciplining reproduction.* Berkeley: University of California Press.

Conly, Verena Andermatt, ed. 1993. *Rethinking technologies.* Minneapolis: University of Minnesota Press.

Corea, Gena. 1985, *The mother machine: Reproductive technologies from artificial insemination to artificial wombs.* New York: Harper and Row.

Cornell, Drucilla. 1995. *The imaginary domain: Abortion, pornography, and sexual harassment.* London: Routledge.

Deleuze and Guattari, preface by Michel Foucault, 1983. *Anti-Oedipus: Capitalism and schizophrenia,* Minneapolis, University of Minnesota Press.

Deleuze, Gilles. 1989. *Masochism: Coldness and cruelty.* New York: Zone Books.

———. 1994. *Difference and repetition.* Trans. Paul Patton. London: Athlone Press.

———. 1997. *Essays critical and clinical.* Trans. Daniel W. Smith and Michael A. Greco. Minneapolis: University of Minnesota Press.

Derrida, Jacques. 1978. *Writing and difference.* Trans Alan Bass. Chicago: University of Chicago Press.

———. 1981(a). *Dissemination.* Trans. Barbara Johnson. Chicago: University of Chicago Press.

———. 1981(b). *Positions.* Trans. Alan Bass. Chicago: University of Chicago Press.

———.1982. *Margins of philosophy.* Trans Alan Bass. Chicago: University of Chicago Press.

———. 1985. *The ear of the other.* Lincoln and London: University of Nebraska Press.

———. 1987(a). *The Postcard,* trans. Alan Bass. Chicago: University of Chicago Press.

———. 1987(b). *Of spirit: Heidegger and the question.* Trans. S. Bennington and Rachel Bowlby. Chicago: University of Chicago Press.

———. 1993. *Aporias: Dying-awaiting (one another at) the "limits of truth."* Trans. Thomas Dutoit. Stanford: Stanford University Press.

———, and Elisabeth Roudinesco. 2004. *For what tomorrow: A dialogue.* Trans. Jeff Fort. Stanford: Stanford University Press.

———.1995. *Gift of death.* Trans. David Wills, Chicago and London: The University of Chicago Press.

Deutscher, Penelope. 2002. *A politics of impossible difference: The later work of Luce Irigaray.* Ithaca: Cornell University Press.

———. 1997. *Yielding gender.* London:Routledge.

Diprose, Rosalyn, and Robyn Ferrell, eds. 1991. *Cartographies: Post structuralism and the mapping of bodies and spaces.* Sydney: Allen and Unwin.

Diprose, Rosalyn. 1994. *The bodies of women: Ethics, embodiment, and sexual difference.* London and New York: Routledge.

———. 2002. *Corporeal Generosities.* New York: State University of New York Press.

Doane, Janice, and Devon Hodges. 1992. *From Klein to Kristeva: Psychoanalytic feminism and the search for the "good enough" mother.* Ann Arbor: University of Michigan Press

Feldstein, Richard, and Judith Roof, eds. 1989. *Feminism and psychoanalysis.* Ithaca: Cornell University Press.

Felman, Shoshana. 1987. *Jacques Lacan and the adventure of insight.* Cambridge: Harvard University Press.

Ferrell, Robyn. 1996. *Passion in theory: Conceptions of Freud and Lacan.* London: Routledge.

———. 2000. "Copula: The logic of the sexual relation." *Hypatia* 15(2).

———. 2002. *Genres of philosophy,* Basingstoke (UK): Ashgate.

Foucault, Michel. 1987. *The history of sexuality.* Trans. Robert Hurley. London: Penguin.

Fox Keller, Evelyn. 1992. *Secrets of life, secrets of death: Essays on language, gender, and science.* New York: Routledge.

Fox, Robin. 1967. *Kinship and marriage : an anthropological perspective.* Harmondsworth : Penguin.

———. 1985. "Conditions of Sexual Evolution." In Aries and Beijin, *Western sexuality: practice and precept in past and present time,* trans. Anthony Forster. Oxford: Blackwell.

Francis, Claude, and Fernande Gontier. 1987. *Simone de Beauvoir: A life . . . a love story.* Trans. Lisa Nesselson. London: Sidgwick and Jackson.

Franklin, Sarah. 1997. *Embodied progress: A cultural account of assisted conception.* London: Routledge.

———. 2000. "Life itself. Global nature and the genetic imaginary." In Sarah Franklin, Celia Lury, Jackie Stacey, *Global nature, Global culture.* London: Sage Publications.

——— 2001. *Culturing biology: Cell lines for the second millennium.* Franklin *Health (London), 2001: 5: 335–54.*

———, and Susan McKinnon. 2001. *Relative values: New directions in kinship study.* London, Durham: Duke University Press.

Freud, Sigmund. 1905. "Three essays on the theory of sexuality." In *Standard edition,* 7, 123. London: Hogarth.

———. 1919. "A child is being beaten." In *Standard edition* 17, 175–204. London: Hogarth.

———. 1924. "The dissolution of the Oedipus complex." In *Standard edition* 19, 173. London: Hogarth.

———. 1933. "Femininity." In *Standard edition* 22, 112. London: Hogarth.

Frow, John. 1998. *Time and commodity culture: Essays on cultural theory and postmodernity.* New York: Oxford University Press.

Fullbrook, Kate and Edward. 1994. *Simone de Beauvoir and Jean-Paul Sartre: The remaking of a twentieth century legend.* New York: Basic Books.

Gallop, Jane. 1985. *Reading Lacan.* Ithaca: Cornell University Press.

Gatens, Moira. 1983. "A critique of the sex/gender distinction." In *Beyond Marxism? Interventions after Marx,* ed. Judith Allen and Paul Patton. Sydney: Intervention. Sydney: Allen and Unwin.

———. 1989. "Woman and her doubles: Sex, gender, and ethics." *Australian Feminist Studies* 10 (Summer): 33–47.

———. 1996. *Imaginary bodies: Ethics, power, and corporeality.* New York: Routledge.

Gilligan, Carol. 1982. *In a different voice.* Cambridge: Harvard University Press.

Grosz, Elizabeth. 1989. *Sexual subversions: Three French feminists.* Sydney: Allen and Unwin.

———. 1990(a). *A feminist introduction.* London and New York: Routledge.

———. 1990(b). "A note on essentialism and difference." In *Feminist knowledge: Critique and construct,* ed. Sneja Gunew. London and New York: Routledge.

———. 1990(c). *Jacques Lacan: A feminist introduction.* London and New York: Routledge.

Haraway, Donna. 1991, *Simians, cyborgs, and women: The reinvention of nature.* New York: Routledge.

———. 1997. *Modest_Witness@Second_Millenium.FemaleMan_Meets_OncoMouseTM: Feminism and technoscience.* New York and London: Routledge.

———. 2003. *The companion species manifesto.* Chicago: Prickly Paradigm Press.

———. 2004. *The Haraway reader.* New York and London: Routledge.

Hegel, G. W. F. 1977. *The phenomenology of spirit.* Trans. A. V. Miller. Oxford: Clarendon Press.

Heidegger, Martin, 1977, *Basic writings.* Ed. David Farrell Krell. London: Routledge.

———. 1984. *The metaphysical foundations of logic.* Trans. Michael Heim. Bloomington: Indiana University Press.

Herlihy, David. 1995. *Women, family and society in Medieval Europe: Historical essays, 1978–1991.* Providence-Oxford: Berghahn Books.

Holmes, H. and L. Purdy, eds. 1992. *Feminist perspectives in medical ethics.* Bloomington/Indianapolis: Indiana University Press.

Hubbard, Ruth. 1990. *The politics of women's biology*. New Brunswick: Rutgers University Press.

Irigaray, Luce. 1985(a). "Commodities amongst themselves." In *This sex which is not one,* trans. Catherine Porter. Ithaca: Cornell University Press.

———. 1985(b). "Cosi fan tutti." In *This sex which is not one,* trans. Catherine Porter. Ithaca: Cornell University Press.

———. 1985(c). "The blind spot of an old dream of symmetry." In *Speculum of the other woman,* trans. C. Gillian. Ithaca: Cornell University Press.

———. 1993(a). *An ethics of sexual difference,* trans. Burke and G. Gill. Ithaca: Cornell University Press.

———. 1993(b). *Je Tu Nous: Toward a culture of difference.* Trans. Alison Martin. New York, London: Routledge.

———. 1994. *Thinking the difference: For a peaceful revolution.* Trans. Karin Montin. London : Athlone Press.

———. 1996. *I love to you.* Trans. Alison Martin. New York, London: Routledge.

Johnson, Barbara. 1977. *The frame of reference: Poe, Lacan, Derrida.* Yale French Studies 55/56:457–508.

Kirkup, Gill, Linda Janes, Kath Woodward, Fiona Hoveden. 2000. *The gendered cyborg A reader.* London and New York: Routledge.

Kristeva, Julia, 1977. *Desire in language. A semiotic approach to literature and art.* Ed. Leon S. Roudiez, trans. Thomas Gora, Alice Jardine, and Leon Roudiez. Oxford: Blackwell.

———. 1986. "Women's Time." In *The Kristeva Reader,* ed. Toril Moi. Oxford: Blackwell.

Lacan, Jacques. 1973. Seminar on "The Purloined Letter." Yale French Studies 48: 39–72.

———. 1977(a). *Ecrits: A selection.* Trans. Alan Sheridan. London: Tavistock.

———. 1977(b). *The four fundamental concepts of psychoanalysis.* Trans. Alan Sheridan. New York: Norton.

Lacy, Nick. 2000. *Narrative and genre.* London: Macmillan.

Laplanche, J. and J-B Pontalis. 1973. *The language of psychoanalysis.* Trans. Donald Nicholson-Smith. London: Norton.

———. 1986. "Fantasy and the Origins of Sexuality." In *Formations of Fantasy,* ed. V. Burgin, J. Donald, and C. Kaplan. London: Methuen.

Lauretis, Teresa de. 1984. "Desire in narrative." In *Alice Doesn't.* Bloomington: Indiana University Press.

———. 1987. *Technologies of gender: Essays on theory, film, and fiction.* London: MacMillan.

Le Doeuff, Michele. 1990. *The philosophical imaginary.* Trans. Colin Gordon. Stanford: Stanford University Press.

———. 1991. *Hipparchia's choice.* Trans. Trista Selous. Oxford: Blackwell.

Levinas, Emmanuel. 1998. *Otherwise than being.* Trans. Alphonso Lingus. Pittsburgh: Duquesne University Press.

———. 1969. *Totality and infinity.* Trans. Alphonso Lingis. Pittsburgh: Duquesne University Press.

Lévi-Strauss, Claude. 1969. *The elementary structures of kinship.* Revised edition, ed. and trans. James Harle Bell, John Richard von Turmer, and Rodney Needham. Boston: Beacon Press.

———. *Structural study of myth.* SA. Vol. 1.

Lloyd, Genevieve. 1984. *The man of reason: "Male" and "female" in Western philosophy.* London: Methuen; Minneapolis: University of Minnesota Press.

———. 1993. *Being in time.* London: Routledge.

Lykke, Nina, and Rosi Braidotti, eds. 1996. *Between monsters, goddesses, and cyborgs: Feminist confrontations with science, medicine, and cyberspace.* London and New Jersey: Zed Books.

McLellan, David. 1975. *Marx.* Glasgow: Fontana/Collins.

MacCannell, Juliet Flower. 2000. *The hysteric's guide to the future female subject.* Minneapolis and London: University of Minnesota Press.

Mackenzie, Adrian. 2002. *Transductions.* London: Continuum.

Mansfield, Nick. 2000. *Subjectivity: Theories of the self from Freud to Haraway.* Sydney: Allen and Unwin.

Marx, Karl. 1971. *The Grundrisse.* Ed. and trans. David McLellan. New York: Harper and Row.

———, and Frederick Engels. 1996. *Collected Works.* London: Lawrence and Wishart.

Maushart, Susan. 1997. *The masks of motherhood: How mothering changes everything and why we pretend it doesn't.* NSW: Vintage Australia.

Merleau-Ponty, Maurice. 1962. *Phenomenology of perception.* Trans. Colin Smith London and New York: Routledge.

Mitchell, Juliet, and Jacqueline Rose. 1982. *Feminine sexuality: Jacques Lacan and the Ecole Freudienne.* London: Macmillan.

Moi, Toril. 1994. *Simone de Beauvoir: The making of an intellectual woman.* London: Blackwell.

Mortley, Raoul. 1991. *French philosophers in conversation.* London: Routledge.

Nicholson, Linda. 1986. *Gender and history: The limits of social theory in the age of the family.* New York: Columbia University Press.

Oliver, Kelly. 1993. *Reading Kristeva: Unravelling the double bind.* Bloomington: Indiana University Press.

———. 1997. *Family values: Subjects between nature and culture.* New York: Routledge.

———. 2001. *Witnessing: Beyond recognition.* Minneapolis and London: University of Minnesota Press.

Olkowski, Dorothea. 1999. *Gilles Deleuze and the ruin of representation.* Berkeley and Los Angeles; University of California Press.

Ollman, Bertell. 1971. *Alienation: Marx's conception of man in capitalist society.* London and New York: Cambridge University Press.

Olson, Gary A., and Elizabeth Hirsh, eds. 1995, *Women writing culture,* Albany: State University of New York Press.

Parisi, Luciana. 2004. *Abstract sex: Philosoph, bio-technology, and the mutations of desire.* London: Continuum.

Pateman, Carole. 1988. *The sexual contract.* London: Polity.

Prokhovnik, Raia. 2002 (2nd ed). *Rational woman: A feminist critique of dichotomy.* Manchester and New York: Manchester University Press.

Purdy, Laura. 1996. *Reproducing persons: Issues in feminist bioethics.* Ithaca: Cornell University Press.

Rich, Adrienne. 1978. *The dream of a common language.* New York: Norton.

———. 1986. *Of woman born: Motherhood as experience and institution.* Tenth Anniversary Edition. New York: Norton.

Roberts, Paul Craig, and Mathew A. Stephenson. 1973. *Marx's theory of exchange, alienation, and crisis.* Stanford: Hoover Institution Press.

Rose, Jacqueline. 1986. *Sexuality in the field of vision.* London: Verso.

———. 1989. "Where does the misery come from? Psychoanalysis, feminism and the event." In *Feminism and Psychoanalysis,* ed. Richard Feldstein and Judith Roof. Ithaca: Cornell University Press.

———. 2003. *On not being able to sleep: Psychoanalysis and the modern world.* Princeton and London: Princeton University Press.

Russell, Bertrand, 1993. *Introduction to mathematical philosophy.* New York: Dover.

Sacher-Masoch, Leopold von. 1997 (5th ed). "Venus in Furs." In *Masochism.* New York: Zone Books

Scharff, Robert, and Val Dusek, eds. 2003. *Philosophy of technology: The technological condition.* Oxford: Blackwell.

Schrader-Frechette, Kristen. 2003. "Technology and ethics." In *Philosophy of technology: The technological condition,* ed. Robert C. Scharff and Val Dusek. Oxford: Blackwell.

Simons, Margaret, ed. 1995. *Feminist interpretations of Simone de Beauvoir.* Pennsylvania: Pennsylvania State University Press.

Sontag, Susan. 1982, c. 1977. "The pornographic imagination." In Lord Auch (Georges Bataille), *Story of the eye,* trans. Joachim Neugroschel, with essays by Susan Sontag and Roland Barthes. Harmondsworth: Penguin.

Spallone, Patricia. 1989. *Beyond conception: The new politics of reproduction.* Massachusetts: Bergin and Garvey.

Spivak, Gayatri. 1989. "Feminism and deconstruction again: Negotiating with unacknoweldged masculinism." In *Between Psychoanalysis and Feminism,* ed. Teresa Brennan. London and New York: Routledge.

Steinberg, Deborah. 1997. *Bodies in glass: Genetics, eugenics, embryo ethics.* Manchester: Manchester University Press.

Stern, Daniel. 1998. *The birth of the mother: How motherhood changes you forever.* London: Bloomsbury Publishing.

Stone, Lawrence. 1977. *The family, sex, and marriage in England 1500–1800.* London: Weidenfeld and Nicolson.

Strathern, Marilyn. 1992. *Reproducing the future: Essays on anthropology, kinship, and the new reproductive technologies.* Manchester: Manchester University Press.

Strouse, Jean. 1985. *Women and analysis: Dialogues on psychoanalytic views of femininity.* Boston: G. K. Hall.

Sullivan, Ellie Ragland. 1989. "Seeking the third term: Desire, the phallus, and the materiality of language." In *Feminism and psychoanalysis,* ed. Richard Feldstein and Judith Roof. Ithaca: Cornell University Press.

Tapper, Marian. 1986. "Can a feminist be a liberal?" *Australasian Journal of Philosophy* 64 Supplement: 37–47.

Throsby, Karen. 2004. *When IVG Fails: Feminism, Infertility and the Negotiation of Normality.* Houndmills: Palgrave.

Tuana, Nancy. 1989. *Feminism and science,* Bloomington: Indiana University Press.

van den Wijngaard, Marianne. 1997. *Reinventing the sexes: The biomedical construction of femininity and masculinity.* Bloomington/Indianapolis: University of Indiana Press.

Vasseleu, Cathryn. 1991. "Life itself." In *Cartographies: Post-structuralism and the mapping of bodies and spaces,* ed. Roslyn Diprose and Robyn Ferrell. Sydney: Allen and Unwin.

Weeks, Jeffrey. 1981. *Sex, politics, and society: The regulation of sexuality since 1800.* London: Longman.

———. 1985. *Sexuality and its discontents: Meanings, myths, and modern sexualities.* London: Routledge.

Wetton, Donn, ed. 1998. *Body and flesh.* Blackwell.

Whitford, Margaret. 1991. *Luce Irigaray: Philosophy in the feminine.* New York, London: Routledge.

Young, Iris Marion. 1990. *Throwing like a girl and other essays in feminist philosophy and social theory,* Bloomington: Indiana University Press.

Ziarek, Ewa Plonowska. 2001. *An ethics of dissensus: Postmodernity, feminism, and the politics of radical democracy.* Stanford: Stanford University Press.

———. 1992. "At the limits of discourse: Heterogeneity, alterity, and the maternal body in Kristeva's thought." *Hypatia* 7 (2) (Spring).

Index of Names